National Symbols at the Olympic Games

This provocative book makes the case for the complete removal of national symbolism in the Olympic Games. Focusing on national flags at the Olympic Games, it explores the history of national symbols at the Olympics and asks what this issue can tell us about the politicisation of sport in the twenty-first century.

Drawing on multi-disciplinary research from history, political science and sociology, and exploring the link between historical processes and the experiences of individuals, the book attempts to deconstruct the global sport system and its traditions. It argues that the history of flags is essentially the history of nationalism itself, impacted by power interests, and by exploring the lesser-known Olympic histories of athletes such as American boxer Oscar De La Hoya or those from the Faroe Islands, the book explores the complex links between national symbolism and international sport. It concludes with a controversial set of proposals for breaking those links, including a new tradition that would symbolically 'lock up' national flags as part of the opening ceremony of Olympic Games.

Thought-provoking and concise, this book is an accessible reading for anybody with an interest in the politics, sociology, history or governance of sport, or in nationalism, international organisations or the history of protest.

Jörg Krieger is Associate Professor at the Department of Public Health at Aarhus University, Denmark. He also holds a Professor II position at University of Inland Norway. He is a sport historian and leads the International Network for Doping Research, the Sport & Society Research Network, and the Lillehammer Olympic and Paralympic Studies Centre.

Routledge Focus on Sport, Culture and Society

Routledge Focus on Sport, Culture and Society showcases the latest cutting-edge research in the sociology of sport and exercise. Concise in form (20,000-50,000 words) and published quickly (within three months), the books in this series represents an important channel through which authors can disseminate their research swiftly and make an impact on current debates. We welcome submissions on any topic within the socio-cultural study of sport and exercise, including but not limited to subjects such as gender, race, sexuality, disability, politics, the media, social theory, Olympic Studies, and the ethics and philosophy of sport. The series aims to be theoretically-informed, empirically-grounded and international in reach, and will include a diversity of methodological approaches.

Available in this series:

Olympic Laws
Culture, Values, Tensions
Mark James and Guy Osborn

Sport and Social Media in Business and Society
Gashaw Abeza and Ryan King-White

Skateboarding and the Senses
Skills, Surfaces, and Spaces
Sander Hölsgens and Brian Glenney

Essentials of Cerebral Palsy Football
Edited by Iván Peña González, Raúl Reina Vaillo, and Manuel Moya Ramón

National Symbols at the Olympic Games
An Olympics Without Flags?
Jörg Krieger

For more information about this series, please visit: https://www.routledge.com/Routledge-Focus-on-Sport-Culture-and-Society/book-series/RFSCS

National Symbols at the Olympic Games

An Olympics Without Flags?

Jörg Krieger

Routledge
Taylor & Francis Group
LONDON AND NEW YORK

First published 2025
by Routledge
4 Park Square, Milton Park, Abingdon, Oxon OX14 4RN

and by Routledge
605 Third Avenue, New York, NY 10158

British Library Cataloguing in Publication Data
A catalogue record for this book is available from the British Library

ISBN: 9781032915869 (hbk)
ISBN: 9781032915876 (pbk)
ISBN: 9781003564058 (ebk)

DOI: 10.4324/9781003564058

Typeset in Times New Roman
by Taylor & Francis Books

Contents

Acknowledgements

I owe my gratitude to a number of people who have supported me during the writing and publication phases of this book. Initial discussions on the history of national flags at the Olympic Games started in 2020 with my former colleague Austin Duckworth. It was a pleasure to work with him on this project in the early stages. Simon Whitmore at Routledge has supported the idea of the book and encouraged me as soon as he received the proposal. I am grateful to John Mason, who helped me strengthen the manuscript. Several friends and colleagues also generously offered their expertise throughout the writing process. Thank you to Peter Lavin, Verner Møller, Ask Vest Christiansen, David Ekdahl, Kristian Raun Thomsen, Anders Schmidt Vinther, Line Wogelius Papp, Peter Ægidiussen Jensen, Allai Abou-Chaker, and my mum Sonja Krieger-Pinnel. All of them had to endure long discussions on the book contents. Finally, I offer my biggest thanks and everlasting love to Eunkyung, Teo, Yuna, and Lily.

Introduction

Can you imagine the Olympic Games without national flags?

Have you considered an Olympic opening ceremony at which athletes march in according to sporting disciplines instead of according to national affiliation? If that is not appealing, how about sorting the athletes by size, hair color, or IQ?

What if all athletes were celebrated by the playing of the Olympic anthem and the raising of the Olympic flag during victory ceremonies? What if athletes could create their own flags or choose a popular song for the victory podium instead of a national anthem?

Have you ever thought of these ideas?

From today's perspective, where national flags play a central and multifaceted role at the Olympic Games, such scenarios appear to be purely hypothetical. In 1968, however, history nearly took a different turn. At a meeting of the International Olympic Committee (IOC), the organization overseeing the staging of the Olympic Games and the international sport system, the question of removal was put up for a vote. The proposal came from the Director of the International Olympic Academy, Prince George of Hanover, who saw in the use of flags at victory ceremonies an "abuse of the Olympic movement towards national and political ends."[1] The majority of IOC members with voting rights agreed with the Prince's argumentation: 34 of 56 individuals voted in favor. However, the proposal was never implemented because it missed out on a two-thirds majority by the small margin of four votes. We almost had an Olympics without flags.

It is idle to speculate about the development the Olympic Games would have taken had four more individuals voted in favor. However, in light of the current challenges international sport is facing due to political conflicts such as those between Ukraine and Russia or Israel and Iran, I feel it is the right time to return to a debate around national symbols in sport. Is it today possible to reverse the decision

DOI: 10.4324/9781003564058-1

of 1968 and organize international sport without those highly politicized national symbols? At the end of this book, I will challenge you to an informed thought experiment that will do exactly that.

Before that, I will deconstruct the use of the nation state concept in international sport that facilitated the inclusion of political symbolism. Then, I will show the paradox of national flag use at the Olympic Games, particularly as sport officials increasingly claimed that sport had to be politically neutral whilst simultaneously allowing for its politicization. Based on this deconstruction, I will then return to the thought experiment in the final chapter and demonstrate how a removal of flags could be implemented.

Current issues in sport

The most pressing issues in international sport are directly connected to national symbolism.[2] First, the participation of Russian athletes in the past ten years often involved banning the Russian flag. Fans recognize the white, blue, and red stripes of Russia's flag. It was prominent at the 2018 Football World Cup in Russia, symbolizing the nation's sporting and political power. However, due to alleged state-sponsored doping, Russian athletes competed as "Olympic Athletes from Russia" under the Olympic flag in 2018. In the 2020 and 2022 Olympics, they used the Russian Olympic Committee (ROC) flag. After Russia invaded Ukraine in February 2022, the IOC allowed Russian and Belarusian athletes to compete under strict conditions, using a new "Individual Neutral Athletes" (AIN) flag. Russian athletes will have competed under four different flags from 2016 to 2024. This highlights the political significance of national symbols in sports, despite claims that sports and politics ought to be kept separate. It also makes any identification of Russian athletes very confusing.

Second, in some instances, sport organizations themselves decided to use national flags to demonstrate sympathies to a cause. Following Russia's invasion of Ukraine, football leagues such as *La Liga* or the *Bundesliga* showed the Ukraine flag during television broadcasts. Ahead of an NBA match in March 2022, the Ukrainian national anthem was performed and the Ukraine flag displayed. German football club Bayern München lit its stadium in Ukraine's colors, and the English Football Association (FA) illuminated Wembley Stadium's arch in yellow and blue. The complexity of such actions became apparent in late 2023, when against the background of the attacks by Hamas militants on Israeli citizens, the FA rejected calls to light up the Wembley arch in colors of the Israeli flag. The issue led to a huge public backlash and the FA then decided that they would no longer light the arch for political or social causes.

Third, increasing global migration, not least reinforced through the recent refugee crisis, has complicated the citizenship-based participation regulations in sport. Athletes, who fled their homelands cannot continue their sporting career without support from the national sport federations in the country in which they hold citizenship. In 2016, the IOC created the Refugee Olympic Athletes (ROA) team, using the Olympic flag, to address this challenge. The IOC argued that the refugees had "no flag, anthem, or home that united them", and regarded the Olympic flag as providing them with a collective identity. Not all refugees were happy with this solution. *Refugee Nation*, a 2015 initiative to establish a refugee nation for stateless individuals,[3] argued that the ROA should have its own flag rather than the Olympic flag that represents all Olympic athletes.[4] *Refugee Nation* adopted its own red-orange flag to symbolize the life vests of refugees fleeing on boats but was unsuccessful with a petition to the IOC.

In addition, political and economic stakeholders are nowadays prepared to buy athletes and players to compete under a new citizenship. 60% of athletes on the Azerbaijan's team at the Rio Summer Olympics in 2016 were foreigners who changed their citizenship to compete under the Azerbaijani flag.[5] In 2022, a Romanian billionaire of Serbian descent sponsored a change of national federation by Hungarian chess player Richárd Rapport, who now competes for Romania.[6] In response to such challenges, some scholars recommended that sport governing bodies should make self-identity the key criteria for allowing athletes to participate for a nation.[7] My own family illustrates this: my three children hold German and South Korean citizenships and can also obtain Danish nationality. Which flag should they compete under should they become elite athletes? Is it fair that only one flag is raised over their heads if they were to be successful in an international sport competition?

Fourth, sport organizations see their sex-segregation system challenged by demands from transgender and intersex athletes. Historically, sports have followed a gender binary, but the rise of the LGBT+ inclusion movement challenges these boundaries. The LGBT+ community has had its own rainbow flag since 1978. Political messages at sports venues have been banned for decades, including rainbow flags. In 2019, the International Triathlon Union banned rainbow flags from races.[8] During the 2014 Winter Olympics in Sochi, Russia banned "propaganda of nontraditional sexual relations," including rainbow flags. However, with more LGBT+ athletes in the Olympics, the IOC now allows them to display the rainbow flag under certain conditions.

Finally, athletes-first movements have grown significantly in recent years. These movements, like *Global Athlete* and the *Centre for Sport and Human Rights*, advocate for individual athletes' rights based on a human rights framework. They have shown that nation-based sport structures can be abused by those in power, who justify their actions through national representation. For example, national sport federations can force athletes to comply with oppressive policies under threat of removal from national teams, essentially asking: flag or be flagged?

In summary, the narrative of political symbols is essential to understand current issues in sport. They are everywhere in sports, and their significance seems to be growing. Even in leagues like the English Premier League, where players represent clubs, players' national flags are shown on TV when the line-ups are presented. It is timely to explore and question the use of flags in sports. While the general history of flags and their meanings to societies has been detailed, much less is known about their use in sports. This book aims to fill this gap.

Flags, this book, and me

There is also a personal connection to the book's topic. National flags do not mean much to me. Yet, out of habit, I have also utilized different national flags in the past to "show my colors". During the 2006 FIFA World Cup in Germany, I was part of the generation who dared to wave the German flag again after the black-red-gold colors had been associated for decades with unhealthy nationalism. I have also waved the Danish flag multiple times during birthday parties in my homeland of choice, as it is an important cultural custom here.

Importantly, I have also been flagbearer myself before. At the 2009 World Championships in Athletics in Berlin, I carried the "Irish tricolor", the national flag of Ireland, into the Olympic Stadium. In contrast to the Olympic Games, the world championships do not feature an athletes' parade with official flagbearers selected by the national federations. Rather, volunteers are selected to carry the national flags. At the time, I had not been aware of the historical significance of my flag-bearing duty. Ireland had boycotted the 1936 Berlin Olympic Games for which the Olympic Stadium had been built. This was the first time that the Irish tricolor was festively paraded into this historically controversial sporting venue for a major multinational sport event. I did not realize that according to sport organizations' understanding of the flag-bearing duty, I became a national symbol myself. "By carrying their national flag during the Parade of Nations, the flagbearer becomes an enduring symbol of their national values," writes the IOC on its website.[9] In other words, on August 15, 2009, I became a national Irish symbol.

I began to question flag use in sport at around the time of the IOC's "punishment" for Russia in removing the nation's national flag from the Olympic Games. Why did the IOC choose a flag removal as disciplinary measure for Russia? In so doing does it not increase the meaning of national symbols and acknowledge that it is the presentation of the political symbol that the nations are "in the game" for?

In this book, I try to find answers for my questions by utilizing an approach anchored in what sociologist C. Wright Mills termed the "sociological imagination". Mills required that any argument should encompass: "history and biography and the relations between the two in society (…) No social study that does not come back to the problems of biography, of history and of their intersections within a society has completed its intellectual journey".[10] Mills thought that an understanding of historical processes was crucial to explain the status quo in society – a description to which international sport policy fits well. However, it was equally important to Mills to comprehend the agency of individuals and personal experiences (biographies) within the context of larger social processes.

The philosopher Zygmunt Bauman, who we will meet at various points throughout this book, understood the task of sociology in a similar manner. He argued that an understanding of personal, real life, individual experiences is the key to revealing a reality that might otherwise remain hidden.[11] It is the task of the social scientists to feed those revelations back to the society and to explain their relevance for the society as a whole.

In practice, when applied in this book, this means zooming into individual circumstances to make current issues in sport properly understandable to the broader public. In doing so, I try to emulate the Dutch writer Geert Mak in filling my historical analysis with personal anecdotes and reflections. Hopefully this allows readers to immerse themselves in the historical events and current debates in global sport.

I am aware that the inclusion of personal experiences and the very particular set of national contexts result in the presented inquiry having a somewhat subjective feel. However, in order to highlight the tensions between flag use, the IOC's claim for political neutrality, and modern athletes' fluid identities, it is necessary to zoom into selected examples to show that the issues presented are deeply resonant with human experience. The range of examples could have easily been expanded to include additional case studies. However, this would have taken away the focus on the in-depth exploration of the contradictions of global sport for individual identity through the history of the flags.

This was also the reason to exclude case studies of ways where the use of national symbols have been used in a positive way to reinforce national identity. For example, the opening ceremony of the London 2012 Olympic Games constructed a specific narrative of the British nation and its history, including many references to the British flag, that was enforced through subsequent newspaper reports on the event.[12] However, even in such cases, scholars have shown that for audiences it is complicated to understand and interpret such narratives.[13] At the 1992 Olympic Games, the event even polarized relations between understandings of nationality identity in Catalonia and Spain.[14]

The earlier parts of the book engage in depth with archival sources collected from newspaper archives in different locations. The historical case studies in the book build in part on archival documentation with a strong emphasis on primary material from the IOC Archive in Lausanne. Finally, newer accounts on ongoing issues with flags use are based on global media and print media extracts, often available online.

The focus on flags in this book is to be understood to be of symbolic nature itself. They become the objects in my argumentation for a larger debate on the use of the nation concept and internationalism in sport. In doing so, my book differs from the vast literature available on the topic of sport and nationalism, particularly from the perspective of sport history. In fact, sport's political history was the first major focus topic for sport historians when the academic field emerged in the 1960s and 1970s. The historiography of sport has evolved over the past decades. However, the issue is as prevalent as ever, and signs of a fundamental readjustment of the interaction between sport and politics are on the horizon.[15] It is time to revisit the relationship between national symbolism and sport.

Notes

1 Minutes, 1968 Session of the International Olympic Committee in Mexico City, October 7–11, 1968, IOC Session Minutes, IOC Historical Archives, Lausanne, 57.

2 Readers should note that the book was finalized before the 2024 Paris Olympic Games and therefore examples from this event are not included.

3 Adam Taylor, "A Silicon Valley mogul wants to solve the global refugee crisis by creating a new country," *Washington Post*, July 23, 2015. https://www.washingtonpost.com/news/worldviews/wp/2015/07/23/a-silicon-valley-mogul-wants-to-solve-the-global-refugee-crisis-by-creating-a-new-country/.

4 Travis Scheadler and Alan Ledford, "Building a Wall Against Refugees: The Refugee Olympic Team & American Politics," *The Sport Journal*, July 18, 2018. https://thesportjournal.org/article/building-a-wall-against-refugees-the-refugee-olympic-team-american-politics/.
5 Gijsbert Oonk, "Sport and Nationality: Towards Thick and Thin Forms of Citizenship," *National Identities* 24, no. 3 (2022): 197–215.
6 Peter Doggers, "Rapport To Switch Federations To Romania; Hungarian Federation 'Protesting'," *Chess.com*, June 19, 2022. https://www.chess.com/news/view/richard-rapport-switch-federations-hungary-romania.
7 Hywel Iowerth, Alun Hardman, and Carwyn Rhys Jones, "Nation, State and Identity in International Sport," *National Identities* 16, no. 4 (2014): 327–47.
8 Cyd Zeigler, "International Triathlon Union bans rainbow flags from all races," *Outsports*, January 18, 2019. https://www.outsports.com/2019/1/18/18188348/rainbow-flag-triathlon-itu-policy-gay-athlete/.
9 "Flying the flag: what it means to be a flagbearer," *Olympics.org*, February 7, 2014. https://olympics.com/en/news/flying-the-flag-what-it-means-to-be-a-flagbearer.
10 C. Wright Mills, *The Sociological Imagination* (Oxford: Oxford University Press, 1959).
11 Zygmunt Bauman, *What Use is Sociology? Conversations with Michael Hviid Jacobsen and Keith Tester.* (Cambridge: Polity Press, 2013).
12 John Vincent, John S. Hill, Andrew Billings, John Harris, and C. Dwayne Massey, "'We are GREAT Britain', British newspaper narratives during the London 2012 Olympic Games," *International Review for the Sociology of Sport* 53, no. 8 (2018): 895–923.
13 Catherine Baker, "Beyond the Island Story?: The Opening Ceremony of the London 2012 Olympic Games as Public History," *Rethinking History* 19, no. 3 (2014): 409–428.
14 John Hargreaves and Manuel Garcia Ferrando, "Public Opinion, National Integration and National Identity in Spain: The Case of the Barcelona Olympic Games," *Nations and Nationalism* 3, no. 1 (1997): 65–87.
15 Julia Neuburg and Lena Overbeck, "Sport & Politik," *ZeitLupe* no. 1 (2024): 6–17.

1 Raising the Flag

Since this book does not present a chronological history of national flags at the Olympic Games but identifies the challenges of flag use and presents alternatives to the current tradition, let me introduce you to the conclusions of my argumentation first.

The first conclusion of this book is that the nation system and flag use in Olympic sports contradict the Olympic Movement's internationalist goals. Therefore, we should consider a removal of national flags and anthems from sporting arenas during competitions to maintain a clear separation between sport and politics. Sport organizations' flags, like the Olympic flag, are not alternatives.

The second key point developed throughout this text is that individual athletes have suffered and will continue to suffer from sport organizations' focus on nations. Therefore, whilst we cannot remove the nation-focused system entirely, athletes should officially be entered in the Olympic Games as individuals. That is, as detached from their nationalities or citizenships as possible.

If we accept the possibility of such a reconstruction of the Olympics' relationship to political symbolism, we can play through the thought experiment of the consequences of such a scenario. I will invite you to run such an exercise in the final chapter of the book. Therein, I question whether the relationship humans have created to particular flags is useful in a sporting context. First, however, I will trace the origins and meanings of "flags" and "nations". These concepts are central to sport today, but what meanings have they had over time? Where do we first find symbols representing a group of people? How was the nation concept understood, and how did flags become attached to it from the seventeenth century onwards?

DOI: 10.4324/9781003564058-1

Flags

> "With a flag you lead men, for a flag, men live and die. In fact, it is the only thing for which they are ready to die in masses, if you train them for it. Believe me, the politics of an entire people … can be manipulated only through the imponderables that float in thin air"[1]

These words by Theodore Herzl, father of modern Zionism, show the psychological impact of political symbolism. For Herzl, writing in the late nineteenth century, the matter was clear. "We have no flag. We need one," he wrote in 1896 in his pamphlet *Der Judenstaat*.[2] The timing of Herzl's considerations is significant for this book. It coincides with the foundation of the modern international sport movement, emphasizing that the concepts of "nation" and "flag" were deeply entrenched in people's minds. The Zionist flag was first displayed internationally at the 1904 St. Louis World Fair, which also hosted that year's Olympic Games.[3]

Herzl's urge to introduce a recognizable symbol for the Jewish people did not come from nowhere. Many nationalistic movements from the eighteenth century onwards displayed national flags and the designs of more than sixty of today's national flags had already emerged by the time of the introduction of the Zionist flag. In fact, the emergence of nationalist sentiments is the history of national flags. Their histories are connected to the constructions of national communities and the creation of nation states all over the world. Here, we see at play what author Yuval Noah Harari identified as *homo sapiens*' unique imaginative capability that allowed us to create myths and believe in things such as nations, religions, rights, or flags.[4]

Flags are a cornerstone of international politics. We take them for granted as we constantly see and engage with them. Flags symbolize the people and the territory of nation states. Flags compress a broad range of meanings, are rich in aesthetic and emotional connotations, and hint at a sense of shared national identity.[5] In an international environment, they express in visual form the fact that the global community is composed of different nations.

But, where did flags come from and how could we become attached to what are essentially pieces of cloth? Symbolism and demarcation have long histories in human cultures. The Ancient Greeks were rumored to use carved standards on the battlefield to send messages to soldiers searching for enemy forces.[6] They might have also used cloth flags as a signal flags and to mark the location of the king in battle. The Romans used the famed eagle standard during battle which "was regarded not merely as a symbol but as a sacred emblem".[7] Flags seem to appear for the first time in the context of war, when opposing forces demonstrated their colors through the usage of flags, to demarcate themselves from others, and to show military divisions the centers of their units.

There are also multiple references to flags, banners and standards in religious works. In the Old Testament's Book of Numbers, Bible readers learn that the Israelites had different "standards" under which they camped during their journey through the desert.[8] The Quran does not directly reference to the use of flags and banners.[9] However, Islamic traditions have seen the use of such symbols in battles. The prophet Muhammad used a black flag as his military flag to distinguish his forces from the adversary's during warfare.[10] Similarly, in the epic Hindu poem Mahabharata, which reached its final form around 400 AD, flags and banners are described in war scenes.

The origin of flags in battle and sacred contexts is an interesting one from a sport history perspective. Sport is also said to have its roots in early warfare and religion. But strikingly, there is no evidence for banners or flags in early sporting competitions. For example, there were no banners or flags at the Ancient Olympic Games to distinguish athletes from the different city states.[11] While the leaders of the modern Olympic Movement never tire of highlighting the Games' Ancient roots, the symbolism attached to it stems from a much later date. It is here that we need to turn towards the concept of the "nation".

The nation

Today, we take it for granted that nations exist that occupy a fixed territory, an efficient administrative structure, loyal citizens, and a national language.[12] However, for the majority of human history, this was not the case and nations did not exist.

Rooted in the Latin term *natio*, used in Ancient Rome to denote communities of foreigners, the concept gained traction in early European academic institutions like the *University of Paris* and *Oxford University* during the thirteenth century to separate student groups by origin.[13] Powerful French Church Council parties adopted the terminology as a synonym for decision-makers and to differentiate themselves from "the people".

At the start of the sixteenth century, the first Tudor King Henry VII accidentally turned the use of the concept on its head.[14] He was forced to recruit aristocrats from outside the traditional upper class, blurring social boundaries. As a result, the strict separation of upper and lower classes began to dissolve. To justify this new form of social mobility, the new elites declared all English people as a "nation", emphasizing equality and inclusion in decision-making. This emergence of one common identity community was nothing less than a revolution in human thinking. By the 1530s this understanding had spread into all aspects of social life in England. The monarchy became intertwined with the collective consciousness of the nation, fostering solidary and shared identity amongst citizens. An "imagined community" of national citizens emerged that spread across Europe, catalyzing the formation of distinct national identities and challenging entrenched monarchical power structures.[15]

The concept of an "imagined community" was developed by political scientist Benedict Anderson.[16] It refers to a socially constructed community, imagined by the people who perceive themselves as part of that group. Members of an imagined community, for example living in the same state, will likely never meet or know most of their fellow members. Despite this, they feel a bond through shared identity, symbols, languages, and narratives, such as those provided by nations and their flags.

The Protestant Reformation of the sixteenth century played a significant role in fostering the notion of nationhood, albeit independently from the emerging national identity in England. The leading reformist Martin Luther challenged existing power structures with support of the newly invented book printing techniques. Prior to this, the Church had monopolized knowledge through Latin, a language accessible only to the educated elite. Luther's dissemination of reformist and subsequently nationalist ideas in vernacular languages empowered individuals across social strata to engage in independent thought. By critiquing the Catholic Church, Luther undermined its authority, paving the way for the acceptance of a unified national identity characterized by shared narratives, events, and ideals.[17]

The French Revolution of 1789 marked a next important turning point. Liberal democratic ideals spread and fostered a collective national consciousness fueled by written accounts of events in Paris.[18] Inspired by the events in France, German intellectuals began to engage in ideas about the overthrow of existing social hierarchies. In parallel, the Napoleonic Wars galvanized German nationalism in opposition to the French, shaping German national identity.[19] The press spread nationalistic rhetoric of outspoken individuals. For example, in 1814 the German scientist Lorenz Oken demanded: "if only one could extirpate the French nation from this earth without ferocity, one would do humanity a big service".[20]

The conflict between the new German and French "nations" points toward a central element of nationhood that we later rediscover in sport: the comparative position of one's nation in relation to others, today known as "international prestige". England with its early understanding of the nation concept took the lead once more. "They no longer could see and experience reality but through the lens of national consciousness, and therefore they imagined they were surrounded by other nations, and thus by competitors", writes historian Liah Greenfeld.[21] However, their European counterparts did at first not share the same competitive drive due to their delayed transformation into nations. By passively looking rather than taking action, they provided the English nation with an advantage and contributed significantly to England's emergence as a global power. By 1850, what then had become the British nation, contributed to the production of more than half of global industrial goods and spread their traditions and ideas – including sports such as cricket, rugby, and football – to all corners of the world. And their flag went with them.

Most prominently, the nation concept sailed with vast numbers of English settlers to the "new world" across the Atlantic Ocean to put down roots in North America. They had a shared consciousness, a national identity. Hence, unlike in Europe, the framework of an American nation preceded the existence of a territory or any social environment. Rather, what is today known as the United States of America "was a *nation*, [and] the only thing that was certain."[22] In other words, the nation idea was deeply entrenched in the creation process and led to the belief that the American nation is purer than any other. Since it took until the end of the nineteenth century for national identities to be created in most other geographical contexts, immigrants to the United States had no *national* awareness and could therefore easily adopt a belief in American national identity.

We know now where the idea of a nation has its origins. However, we still need to know how the nations began to organize themselves as states and began to interact with each other. The Peace of Westphalia in 1648 is usually cited as the starting point for such international relations. The Peace ended the Thirty Years' War as the parties decided to create a global order based on nation states. Since the European powers, including Britain through its empire, spread the idea to other parts of the world, the nation state model became the blueprint for all international systems. The system aimed to create peace amongst nations, but did not dictate to new members how to adjust their internal affairs. Any emerging state simply had to acknowledge that international affairs took place between nation states. As such, the Westphalian system, which today still provides the main structure in the international system, did not create one centre of power but took diversity as a starting point.[23]

National flags

How then did flags become attached to nations, triggering meanings and emotions for their citizens?

Though the Peace of Westphalia made no specific mention of national flags, these symbols naturally emerged as distinctive markers for the new key agents in global affairs. We return to Great Britain and the new nation's competitiveness to find the roots of national flag use. From the sixteenth century onwards English and Scottish trading ships used flags to signal their origins. The English featured a red St. George's cross on a white background whereas the Scottish flag displayed a white St. Andrew's saltire against blue.[24] As such, royal emblems lost in significance as they represented the monarchy, whereas regular citizens began to identify as a nation and began to search for their own new "national" symbols.

When in 1649, the British monarchy was abolished and a Commonwealth with a sovereign and written constitution was declared, it adopted a flag containing the St. George's cross, the St. Andrew's saltire, and in some versions the gold harp of Ireland.[25] Whilst the Commonwealth was a failure and in 1660 the monarchy restored, its legacies flattered on.

The roots of the black-red-gold flag lie in anti-Napoleonic sentiment and efforts to create German unity. Politicians and journalists fostered national identity in the 1830s, culminating in the Hambacher Festival where the flag gained prominence. Despite resistance, it became known as the "German flag" by 1832.[26] "High fly the German colors," sang the revolutionaries and continued: "The variety of colors are Germany's distress. United strength alone begets greatness. So away with the variety of colors! Only one color and one fatherland."[27] We see here the beginning of how groups tried to trigger emotions through symbols and how they began to instrumentalize the link between flags (colors) and national causes.

Regional identities initially conflicted with the flag's adoption, as seen in a south-west German newspaper. "As if without those colors (…), we could not be German anymore," wrote the author.[28] It was not until 1848 that the German Empire officially adopted the black-red-gold flag, symbolizing the first attempt at constitutional unity. Such regional hesitation still exists in Germany today, particularly in the South. In Bavaria, you are much more likely to come across the white and blue Bavarian lozenge flag than the German national flag. Local right-wing parties even label the German flag, the symbol of the "occupying forces".

The emergence of the German nation and its flag is only one example of how the notion of the nation state became increasingly apparent in global politics.[29] Grass-roots movements all shared the idea to create larger communities and liberal ideas about free nations and the freedom of the individual. The advocates for national identities argued that each people had its cultural unity, which manifested itself especially in a common language, history, and territory.[30] National flags, together with other symbols and celebrations, became central to creating such a sense of community. However, when the shared cultural unity was transformed into a political reality in the form of a nation state, the symbolism of flags merged with political meanings.

The nation concept symbolized through flags was further complicated towards the middle of the nineteenth century when what then became known as "nationalism" evolved from a popular sovereignty advocating political ideology to a right-wing movement. In other words, a rhetoric of "us" versus "them" emerged, and the nation idea became increasingly ambiguous: while rooted in democracy, nationalism became loaded with ideas of national superiority and aggression towards others. Ironically, both old monarchies and new nation rulers now began to use nationalism as a form of propaganda to "unify" their citizens for causes.[31] The term "nation" now emphasized the absolute primacy of one's own nation externally, while internally, it was characterized by exclusive definitions of national identity. Hence, even though national flags had only just emerged in international trade, the complexity of their symbolism grew with them.

Yet again the German flag is illustrative since its initial black-red-gold stripes did not at first survive politically unstable times. There were simply too many small nation states in Germany to be united under one banner.[32] In 1871, the Imperial German Flag, consisting of black-white-red stripes, became Germany's new political flag since the new leadership rejected revolutionary symbolism. The Nazi flag further complicated the relationship between German citizens and their national flags in the second half of the twentieth century. Such inconsistencies and continuous renegotiations of the relationship between state, nation, and flag in Germany have caused an emotional distance between national flags and citizens in the country.[33] When during the 2006 Football World Cup hundred thousands of young Germans, including myself, celebrated in black-red-gold colors, older generations confusingly looked on and the flag finally became a more commonly used symbol in the country.

Irrespective of the admittedly special German case, it is evident that flags as political symbols were beginning to be imbued with emotions and political significance throughout the nineteenth century. The ethnologist Orvar Löfgren argues "as flags were nationalized they acquired new magical powers (...). The very fact that the flag is alive and moving also stresses its emotional impact, its ability to move people".[34] According to Löfgren, flags have the ability to transmit strong meanings to the individual members of the group that adopt the symbol as theirs.[35] This psychological impact was vividly illustrated in 2024 when Apple faced a backlash for automatically displaying a Palestinian flag emoji for users typing "Jerusalem," igniting strong national sentiments tied to the Israeli-Palestinian conflict.

In the United States, national identity predated the birth of the state. Even today, patriotic flag-waving Americans are "reaping nationalism".[36] The United States' first flag, then already consisting of alternate red and white stripes and stars in a blue field, was introduced in 1777 as a naval flag following the maritime traditions prevalent in European contexts. It became a symbol of national identity during the American Civil War when a surrendered stars and stripes flag was used to raise war funds in the Northern states and steer nationalistic sentiments.[37] Since then, countless groups in the United States have usurped the flag and attempted to attach radical meanings to it. In her political history *Capture the Flag*, the scholar Woden Teachout concludes that overall a historical shift occurred from the US flag as humanitarian symbol to a predominantly nationalistic one in the twenty-first century. In short, the American flag is today more political than ever.

Such historical viewpoints are confirmed in studies on the psychological impact of flags on national identity. One study shows that even short exposure to a nation's flag, in this case the Israeli flag, can impact the political opinions of respondents.[38] In short, national flags have today acquired the ability to communicate an identity, to represent collectiveness, and at times to serve aggressive political positioning. Not only in the United States, Germany, or Great Britain, but worldwide.

National flags fly outside the West

Until now, I have focused only on the emergence of flags and nations in a Western European context. In this sub-section, we will take a global roundtrip to expand our perspective and to comprehend how the interpretation and use of flags impacted modern, perceptions of national symbolism rooted in the West.

South America is our first destination. Initially, the European colonizers had brought their national flags with them from the late fifteenth century onwards. In the nineteenth century, South American colonies sought independence, influenced by Western liberal ideals. Leaders like Simón Bolívar and José de San Martín used flags to symbolize their movements and to demarcate their groups from the colonializing forces. During the Chilean War of Independence in 1817, light-blue and white flags were prominent.[39] Those colors continue to provide the basis for the national flags of Uruguay and Argentina today. Contemporary South American flags often feature designs inspired by independence movements, known as "flags of freedom".[40] Thus, even though the flags themselves had their origins in colonial rule, the new nations adopted the tradition.

Across the Pacific Ocean in East Asia, national flags emerged with Westernization and independence movements. Japan adopted the Hinomaru flag in 1870 after the Meiji Restoration.[41] China introduced a national flag after the Qing Dynasty's fall in the early twentieth century. Korea's flag gained prominence during its struggle for independence from Japan in the 1930s and 1940s. Vietnam declared independence from France in 1945, adopting a red flag with a gold star, symbolizing Communism. After the Vietnam War and reunification in 1976, this flag became the national symbol, representing socialist and communist ideologies in various contexts, including sports.

A sea journey across the India Ocean takes us to the African continent, where decolonization took place mainly in the second half of the twentieth century. By that time, the nation concept had become so widespread as a means to organize global order that all African liberation movements were marked by the desire to establish independent nations. Ghana became the first sub-Saharan African country to gain independence from colonial rule in 1957. In that year, Ghana adopted its own national flag with three horizontal red-yellow-green stripes and a black five-pointed star in the center. Ghana's flag, like the majority of formerly colonialized African nations has its roots in a pan-Africanist flag. Pan-Africanism, which refers to various movements in Africa that aimed to eliminate colonialism and white supremacy from the continent is another excellent example, focused on the creation of nations, the paradoxically, Western and colonialist construct. Interestingly, the creator of Pan-African flag, Marcus Garvey, thought that the flag should be a flag for all people of the Black race, considering it to represent people beyond a particular nation. However, since the global political and sporting systems foresaw an organization of the world into nations, the new countries had to pick a national flag.[42]

In the North, the nineteenth century Russian Empire, under an autocratic rule, used a white-blue-red tricolor flag designed by Czar Peter the Great, inspired by the Netherlands. The flag symbolized oppression for many ethnic groups within the empire, leading to nationalist pressures. The 1917 Russian Revolution established the Soviet Union, replacing the old flag with socialist symbols. After the Soviet Union dissolved in 1991, the Russian flag re-emerged amid struggles to define national identity. Under Vladimir Putin, Russia has emphasized nationalism and traditional values, viewing the flag as a symbol of shared historical, cultural, and linguistic roots.

Nations that emerged from former ethnic groups first included in the Russian Empire and then in the Soviet Union actively used national flags to distinguish themselves from Russia. For example, in the 1990s, all three Baltic states reinstated the distinctive pre-Soviet flags upon regaining independence that had been used as symbols of national identity prior to Soviet occupation. Countries such as Poland, the Czech Republic and Hungary, which were under strong control of the Soviet Union, similarly succeeded in promoting a separate national identity, even though they faced internal national and ethnic tensions. An exception was Yugoslavia, where various ethnic groups pulled in different directions in their attempts to nationalize. The result was a brutal civil war in which national flags became very widespread symbols of identity, allegiance, and sovereignty, reflecting the complex ethnic and nationalist dynamics at play in the region.

The last destination of our global journey returns us to the beginning of this chapter, the Middle East. Here, the French and British colonizers prioritized their interests in the region, particularly their access to oil. The 1916 Sykes-Picot Agreement created artificial national borders, forming protectorates like Iraq, Syria, Lebanon, and Jordan. These borders divided ethnic communities, causing tensions and conflicts. Nationalist movements arose as these regions gained independence, adopting national flags symbolizing their struggles. For example, Egypt's flag, adopted in 1952 after the revolution, includes a black stripe to represent overcoming foreign imperialism. These developments reflect the influence of colonialism on Middle Eastern national identities and symbols.

In sum, considering the rising significance of national symbolism all over the globe throughout the nineteenth and twentieth century, it is perfectly understandable that Theodor Herzl strove for the introduction of a Zionist flag in the late nineteenth century. Flags now had the ability to convey messages and meanings under the name of nationalism that transcended language boundaries. Nations and their flags became the main signifiers during this time, and this is crucial to understand as the international sport movement emerged in parallel at the turn to the twentieth century. National flags were the obvious symbol to include in the competitions to demarcate athletes from each other.

However, our trip around the world also demonstrates that the problems with the use of national flags grew exponentially. Over time, the symbols became more nationalist, more politicized, more aggressive, and more meaningful for oppressed groups. Cultural meanings became replaced by political meanings, and national flags now represent the power balances and political ideologies at the time they were adopted. They also did and do not necessarily speak for all citizens.

Conclusion

Imagine the creation of a new nation. A nation without a flag. Could such a nation be taken seriously in our day? How would it be represented amongst all other nations that use flags? Most likely, it would be regarded as an empty nation, laughed about. However, the link between flags and nations was not a given. Rather, the tradition of national symbols spread via the most advanced nations throughout the globe.

Flags have always been associated with conflict. Inner-group togetherness emerged only in opposition to other societal groups in violent encounters from the French Revolution to the Yugoslav Wars. They became instrumentalized when the nation concept emerged, and heavily politicized in parallel with nationalist movements. Any discussion about national flags is today heavily emotional and extreme. This can be seen in the various attempts in the United States to legislate about establishing penalties for the physical destruction of the US national flag, for example by burning it. Similarly, in South Korea, the National Security Act forbids the display of the North Korean flag – even though there are some exceptions for cultural events such as sporting competitions.[43]

We have also seen that regimes all over the world claimed ownership over far-flung territories by using their flag.[44] From Argentina to St.

Petersburg, revolutionaries and powerholders created flags to signal a new beginning, break-ups with oppressing traditions, or a resurrection of past power structures. Flags represented a nation's permanence and their people's right to sovereignty. Thus, flags have always been associated with conflict, later acquiring meaning for individuals attached to them, representing a shared consciousness amongst a particular group, and finally becoming heavily politicized. As such, national flags and banners stand in stark contrast to the internationalism that the modern sport movement promotes.

The "international" nature of sport is precisely the crux of the matter here, since it is here that national flags are most prominently used. However, rather than stating the obvious, namely that the use of national flags means that sport is about politics, sport organizations argue the opposite. As we will see in the next chapter, the foundation of and current justifications for the modern sport system are deeply rooted in a liberal rhetoric that claims to promote peace.

Against the historical background I have sketched out, I shall be referring to the nation state when I speak about nations, states, or countries over the next chapters. To me, that is the assumed alignment between the cultural entity of the nation and the political/territorial unit of the state.[45] Accordingly, I refer to national flags as the visible symbol of a nation state that have generated an awareness of national boundaries and fostered a collective national identity.[46]

Notes

1 Robert Justin Goldstein, *"Saving Old Glory": The History Of The American Flag Desecration* (Abingdon: Routledge, 2019).
2 Herzl's own suggestion of a white flag with seven golden stars was never realized as the Zionist movement, and later the State of Israel, adopted a blue and white flag with the Star of David printed upon it.
3 Keith Feldman, "Seeing Is Believing: U.S. Imperial Culture and the Jerusalem Exhibit of 1904," *Studies in American Jewish Literature* 35, no. 1 (2016): 98–118.
4 Yuval Noah Harari, *Sapiens. A Brief History of Humankind* (New York: Random House, 2011).
5 Thomas Hylland Eriksen, "Some questions about flags," In *Flag, Nation and Symbolism in Europe and America*, eds. Thomas Hylland Eriksen and Richard Jenkins, (Abingdon: Routledge, 2007), 7.
6 J.A. Richmond, "Spies in Ancient Greece," *Greece & Rome* 45, no. 1 (1998): 1–18.
7 Willie Thompson, *Work, Sex and Power: The Forces That Shaped Our History.* (London: Pluto Press, 2015).
8 4 Mose 1, 52.

9 Mustazah Bahari and Muhammad Haniff Hassan, "The Black Flag Myth: An Analysis from Hadith Studies," *Counter Terrorist Trends and Analyses* 6, no. 8 (2014): 15–20.
10 It was only during the Abbasid movement around 750 CE that the black flag became an "official" flag for the caliphate.
11 Nigel B. Crowther, "The Ancient Olympic Games," in *Olympic Knowledge – Essential Reading Series*, ed. The Olympic Studies Centre (Lausanne: The Olympic Studies Centre, 2024), 1–13.
12 Chris Harman, *A People's History of the World* (Brooklyn: Verso, 2017), 172.
13 Oliver J. Thatcher, *The Library of Original Sources* (London: University Research Extension, 1901), 380.
14 Liah Greenfeld, *Nationalism. A Short History* (Washington D.C.: The Brookings Institution, 2019), 14.
15 Luke Cooper, "Imagined communities: from subjecthood to nationality in the British Atlantic," *International Relations* 37, no. 1 (2023): 72–95.
16 Benedict Anderson, *Imagined Communities. Reflections on the Origin and Spread of Nationalism* (Revised Edition) (London: Verso, 2006).
17 Alexander Betts, *Forced Migration and Global Politics* (London: Wiley-Blackwell, 2009).
18 Anderson, *Imagined Communities*, 80.
19 Greenfeld, *Nationalism*, 92.
20 Klaus Ries, "Lorenz Oken als politscher Professor der Universität Jena," *in Lorenz Oken, ein Politischer Naturphilosoph,* ed. Olaf Breidbach, Hans Joachim Fliedner, and Klaus Ries (Weimar: Verlag Hermann Böhlaus, 2001), 96.
21 Greenfeld, *Nationalism*, 22.
22 Liah Greenfeld, *Nationalism. Five Roads to Modernity* (Cambridge: Harvard University Press, 1992), 402.
23 Henry Kissinger, *Weltordnung* (München: C. Bertelsmann, 2014), 39.
24 John Cartledge, "Flags and Emblems of the British Republic 1649–1660, in *Proceedings of the 25th International Congress of Vexillology*, 4–10 August 2013, accessed June 7, 2024, https://fiav.org/wp-content/uploads/2021/06/ICV2501-John-Cartlegde-Flags-and-emblems-of-the-British-Republic-1649-1660.pdf.
25 Ibid.
26 *Schwäbischer Merkur*, June 19, 1932, accessed via *Deutsches Zeitungsportal*, https://www.deutsche-digitale-bibliothek.de/newspaper.
27 Paul Wentzcke, "Der Deutschen Mai 1832 Voraussetzung, Verlauf und Folgen des Hambacher Festes," *Aus Politik und Zeitgeschichte* 19 (1957), 1–4.
28 *Karlsruher Zeitung*, June 30, 1832, accessed via *Deutsches Zeitungsportal*, https://www.deutsche-digitale-bibliothek.de/newspaper.
29 Christopher Bayly, *The Birth of the Modern World 1780–1914* (Oxford: Blackwell Publishing, 2004).
30 John P. McKay, *A History of World Societies* (Boston: Bedford, 2009).
31 Harman, *A People's History.*
32 The same problem occurred on the Italian peninsula.
33 Enrico Brissa, *Flagge zeigen! Warum wir gerade jetzt Schwarz-Rot-Gold brauchen* (München: Siedler Verlag, 2021).
34 Orvar Löfgren, "A Flag For All Occasions? The Swedish Experience," In *Flag, Nation and Symbolism in Europe and America*, eds. Thomas Hylland Eriksen and Richard Jenkins, (Abingdon: Routledge, 2007), 138.

35 Robert Shanafelt, "The Nature of Flag Power," *Politics Life Science* 27, no. 2 (2008): 13–27.
36 Markus Kemmelmeier and David G. Winter, "Sowing Patriotism, But Reaping Nationalism? Consequences of Exposure to the American Flag," *Political Psychology* 29 (2008): 859–879.
37 Oliver Williams Black, "The 150-Year War: The Struggle to Create and Control Civil War Memory at Fort Sumter National Monument," *The Public Historian* 38, no. 4 (2016): 149–166.
38 Orla T. Muldoon, Karen Trew, and Paula Devine, "Flagging difference: Identification and emotional responses to national flags," *Journal of Applied Social Psychology* 50, no. 5 (2020): 265–275.
39 Peter Blanchard, *Under the Flags of Freedom: Slave Soldiers and the Wars of Independence in Spanish South America* (Pittsburgh: University of Pittsburgh Press, 2008).
40 Ibid., 1.
41 Jürgen Osterhammel, *Die Verwandlung der Welt: Eine Geschichte des 19. Jahrhunderts* (München: C. H. Beck, 2009), 26.
42 Tim Marshall, *A Flag Worth Dying For. The Power and Politics of Flags* (New York: Schribner, 2016), 208.
43 Jonathan Leib and Gerald Webster, "Rebel with(out) a cause? The contested meanings of the Confederate battle flag in the American South," in *Flag, Nation and Symbolism in Europe and America*, eds. Thomas Hylland Eriksen and Richard Jenkins, (Abingdon: Routledge, 2007), 32.
44 Eric Hobsbawm, *The Invention of Tradition* (Cambridge: Cambridge University Press, 1983), 11–12.
45 Betts, *Forced Migration*, 43.
46 Daron Acemoglu and James A. Robinson, *Why Nations Fail: The Origins of Power, Prosperity, and Poverty* (New York: Currency, 2012), 80.

2 Internationalism, Flags, and the Olympics

> What has made sport so uniquely effective a medium for inculcating national feelings, at all events for males, is the ease with which even the least political or public individuals can identify with the nation (…). The imagined community of millions seems more real as a team of eleven named people. The individual, even the one who only cheers, becomes a symbol of his nation himself.[1]

The quote above stems from the influential social and economic historian Eric Hobsbawm. He lived in Vienna between 1931 and 1933 as a teenager during a time when the football team Rapid Vienna, and Austria in general, emerged as a dominant force in European football. It is likely that Hobsbawm knew about Rapid, even more so since he apparently had a picture of a 1930s Rapid team in his hallway. However, considering that the small paragraph above is amongst only a few statements that Hobsbawm made about sport, we can confidently say that he was not a passionate follower of football or any other sport.

As one of the most brilliant historians of our time, Hobsbawm understood and could explain in a few sentences that sport today serves as a powerful tool for fostering national identity amongst citizens. He captured the idea that nations find expression through popular sporting events and individuals, alongside other significant national symbols like the military. Athletes, much like soldiers, embody and represent their nations when competing, contributing to contests for national supremacy. Following Hobsbawm's argument, a young German volunteer carrying the Irish flag into Berlin's Olympic Stadium became a symbol of the Irish nation.

National flags are omnipresent in international sport and therefore observers can learn about political ideologies at sport events. Take the

DOI: 10.4324/9781003564058-2

national flags of the Asian countries of China, Vietnam, Laos, or North Korea which all contain Communist symbols. Angola, Cuba, Mozambique, and Zimbabwe are also examples. The presence of these symbols does not necessarily mean that the country is currently governed by a Communist regime, but they might be understood as expressing Communism's intolerance towards alternative political viewpoints. In contrast, no symbolism related to capitalism as a political ideology is displayed in sporting arenas via a national flag since none currently contains explicit any symbolism of capitalism.

Mozambique's flag is a particularly ambivalent example. It shows a Kalashnikov AK-47 assault rifle with a bayonet attached to it and is the only national flag with a modern weapon in it. The flag was prominently visible to the international community at the 2000 Olympic Games when 800-meter runner Maria Mutola won the nation's first Olympic gold medal. To Mozambiquans, the rifle represents defence and vigilance, but should such symbolism be visible in a sporting event promoting world peace? It appears that the Mozambiquan sport movement is very well aware of the contrast: the flag of the nation's NOC includes a torch based on the Olympic torch. However, that flag is not seen internationally, as sport opted for political rather than sporting symbols.

Internationalism

Internationalism is the political practice whereby different nations or states cooperate with each other.[2] It is to be differentiated from internationalization, which refers to the process of growing relations across borders and between states. International organizations are one result of these two concepts as they were created as formal institutions by nations or their representatives to achieve shared objectives on a global scale.

Tracing the genealogy of the term "international" is useful here. We already learned that the English after developing the concept of a nation, began to compete with other nations to preserve their national dignity during the late seventeenth century.[3] Due to England's status as the first global superpower, other emerging nations were forced to compete in the areas that the English engaged in. Any external contact between nations, "inter-national" contact, was based on the aim to symbolize a nation in trade, protect one's own nation, or flag, and show strength.

The word "international" was not widespread in Europe until the middle of the nineteenth century. Only from the 1860s onwards, did newspaper writers in Britain use the term regularly. Since then, the appearance of "international" is recorded more than a million times in the British Newspaper Archive. In Denmark, readers come across the words for the first time in the early 1840s in the context of trade and questions of an "international law" to conduct business.[4] A German newspaper defined "international" as "encompassing all European nations" in 1825.[5] The timing is interesting since, as we learned earlier, an understanding of Germany as a nation was still in its infancy. Five years later, another German newspaper used the word to describe bloodlines that moved from one nation to another.[6]

The idea of a peaceful existence *between* and *with* other nations emerged in North America and Britain during the 1810s when peace societies, commonly known as "friends of peace", were founded. Such initiatives, like others that followed mainly in Europe, did not entail the creation of a "world state or world federation" in the sense of an internationalization.[7] Rather, internationalism was the focus with the aim to form an international law. Utilitarian philosopher Jeremy Bentham coined the understanding of the term "international" in such fashion.[8]

Critical scholars argue that early peace efforts were also "shot through with inequalities of gender and political representation".[9] For example, the International Council of Women, as a prominent international non-state actor, founded in 1899, focused on internationalism. Beliefs such as women's right to political participation crossed borders. Groups of individuals could influence international relations through their actions, decisions, and interactions, irrespective of their national boundaries.

The contradictions in all above viewpoints are best illustrated in the support for the peace movement and internationalism from Russian Czar Nicholas II. American newspapers considered the Czar an individual with shattered nerves, without much will of his own.[10] A powerful man, who for his time and position unusually strongly influenced by the actions and beliefs of his wife and his mother.[11] Nicholas II was particularly fond of Russian writer Leon Tolstoy with whom he also maintained a written correspondence. Tolstoy, of course, was a strong critique of national boundaries and a strong promoter of pacifism. He had an impact on Nicholas' initiative for the First Hague Peace Conference in 1899 at which 26 nation states discussed peace and an international jurisdiction. Six years later, the Czar again sent invitations to a follow-up conference. This time representatives of 44 countries answered his call.

What were Nicholas' motives? Did he blindly follow Tolstoy's opinions as he handed over his reins of power to his wife? Russian tsarism had long been a force countering revolutionary development in Europe and had turned to capitalism to finance military expansion amidst the threat of revolutions.[12] Hence, it is unlikely that Tolstoy's parables were the main driving force behind the Czar's activity. His autocratic rule over Russia was not a reflection of liberal governance. His interest in the peace movement was instead driven by the fear of defeat.[13] The pacifist Bertha von Suttner commented about the Czar's second peace conference: "it was not a conference about peace, but about the customs of war."[14] A few years later she reflected: "The peace movement and the craze for armament seem to keep pace in progressing. The more Hague Conferences, the more war taxes."[15] Internationalist efforts were off to a bad start.

Other peace movements also maintained a focus on the collaboration between nation states. Two years after a Universal Peace Congress in Paris in 1889, the International Peace Bureau (IPB) was established in Berne, Switzerland. The IPB was a mediation center that aimed to solve potential disputes between nations peacefully by having states sign up to mutual arbitration laws. Other initiatives like the Nobel Peace Prize, first awarded in 1901, focused on promotion of peace and cooperation outside a nation state framework. There were overlaps, of course. For example, the IPB received the Nobel Peace Prize in 1910. What these initiatives did have in common, however, was that they were all international efforts initiated in Europe and based on the nation state originating in the West and co-produced by Europe's imperial power structures.[16]

I urge you therefore to consider those important nuances in the history of internationalism. If you do so, you must side with those historians who have pointed out that internationalism has been influenced by specific national political, ideological or regional agendas.[17] For example, Western powers had wanted to maintain influence over their colonies and shape a world order according to their own interests. Within internationalist and peace movements, there were differing views on neutrality with some arguing for strict non-involvement while others thought active invention was necessary to protect human rights. Even the League of Nations reflected the interests of the dominant powers and was therefore not politically neutral. This finding is significant as the global sport movement adopted the same internationalist, but originally not politically neutral, discourse from its days of infancy.

Sport, flags, internationalism

The idea of sport between nation states is as modern a cultural invention as international collaboration on the political level. The spread of sport has its roots in industrial Great Britain, where it was first used as an educational tool at public schools. When the upper-class, male graduates left their schools, they planted sport at universities and often maintained their enthusiasm for competition when they took on important military, religious, or political roles.[18]

An overlooked example of such an impactful individual is Charles W. Alcock. Born in 1842, he was a graduate of the Harrow Public School. At this educational institution for upper class boys, Alcock got fascinated by the game of football. After graduation, he founded Wanderers F.C. at the age of only seventeen to promote his interest and spread the game's competitive nature. Alcock was also influential in the formation of the modern-day federation structures in sport as he founded the English Football Association (FA) in 1863 and became the organization's secretary a few years later. In this capacity, he created the Football Association Challenge Cup, the world's first knockout sport competition.

In view of such merits, it is understandable that newspapers describe Alcock as enthusiastic and passionate.[19] And he had more ideas up his sleeve. It was Alcock who initiated the first international football matches between teams from England and Scotland in the early 1870s. A few games between an English and a Scottish club had taken place before, but the teams were put together irrespective of nationality. This changed with Alcock's proposal to have an annual match between two separate teams solely composed of players from the same nation. The idea of national teams was born.

There is no evidence for national flags present at the first England versus Scotland matches, but the teams' outfits represented the colors of England (white) and Scotland (dark blue). The English had a badge of the three lions on their shirts, the logo adopted by Alcock's FA. The lions are also present on England's royal coat of arms, dating back to King Richard I in the twelfth century. As we learned in Chapter 1, it was such aristocratic ties that national movements later overthrew. The same is true for the Scottish badge on the shirts in 1872, which was the Royal Banner of Scotland. The logos of both football associations today are still based on the banners. The many people who express their *national* sense of belonging through the respective football teams are actually being duped. The logos present precisely what a nation has rejected.

International sport, like the United Nations, can be traced to the unfulfilled desire for harmony and peace.[20] However, because like early efforts promoting peace, the concept was doomed from the start: international sport was marked by competitiveness rather than collaboration. In fact, ideas of peaceful interaction are absent from all of Alcock's writings and public statements on football matches between nations. Therefore it is not surprising that the scholar John Hoberman recognized that "internationalist projects of this period were not negations of nationalism but rather cultural projections of nationalist impulses employing cosmopolitan vocabularies rooted in ethnocentric ideas of national grandeur."[21]

Precisely such demonstrations of national characteristics at sporting contests brought the flags "into the game". It is not coincidental that when sporting pastimes that have their origins in 19th century Britain started to flourish around the globe, flags as symbols of modern nationhood would start to appear regular in conjunction with sporting events. They were markers or dividers, not connectors. Uniforms/kits, logos, flags, and anthems began to contribute to representing the nation in sport and mark differences in cultural histories.

The first international contests

Before Alcock's international football match, there were a few isolated international sporting exchanges that have connections to national symbolism. Most commentators cite the 1844 cricket match between two teams from the USA and Canada at the St. George's Cricket Club in Manhattan as the beginning of international competitions in North America.[22] The American club had issued a challenge "to play any 11 in Canada for any amount, from 100 to 1000 dollars," to find out which nation had the better cricket players.[23] A Toronto-based team responded, confidently agreeing to play for the highest proposed sum. There are no images of the match. Reports of the event, however, often use a drawing from the Museum of the City of New York to add a visual feature to the descriptions. At the center of the drawing stands a flagpole bearing the star-spangled banner. A flag representing Canada, which would have been the British Union Jack since Canada had not been founded yet, is absent. One should not be fooled by the image though. The drawing is in fact from a year earlier and can therefore not display the contest between the Americans and the Canadians. We can therefore not conclude that national flags were used to symbolize the two opposing teams. Rather, it is likely that the flagpole generally played a central role at the cricket ground, which is hardly surprising considering the ongoing efforts in the United States to create national unity at the time.

It would take until after the turn to the twentieth century for international football matches to be contested outside the British Isles. In 1902, Uruguay and Argentina met in Montevideo for the first football game between two independent nations. The match is of significance because it is here that for the first time we find a national flag on an official photograph of an international football match. On the image portraying the Uruguayan starting eleven, the "Sun and Stripes" national flag is held by one of the players. The flag's appearance is certainly an indication of an early formation of national identity through football in Uruguay.[24] Much of the identity formation is a result of its footballing rivalry with Argentina, even though the nations share the same history of native South Americans fighting against Spanish colonialism.

On the European mainland, a match between an Austrian and a Hungarian team was later awarded the right to claim the first national match. It also took place in 1902. At the time of the event, the game was contested between teams from the cities of Vienna and Budapest, both part of the Austro-Hungarian dual monarchy, and therefore no flags were flown at the game.[25] The Hungarian team's captain was twenty-four-year-old Alfred Hajós. This was Hajós' only international football appearance and we will learn shortly that his story is deeply connected to sport, national symbolism and its challenges.

In sum, we learn that the emergence of international sport contests, particularly in football, was not tied to national symbolism at the beginning of the twentieth century. Specifically designed logos and sporting symbols were used instead. These could also be seen at the first European match between two independent nations that took place two years later in 1904 between teams from France and Belgium. Both teams played in their national colors, with the French jerseys displaying the logo of the Union of French Athletic Sports Society, not the national flag.[26] How then did the nation and its flag become so deeply embedded in global sport?

Olympic internationalism

The short answer is through the policies of the International Olympic Committee (IOC). It was the IOC that institutionalized sport and required the use of national flags at sporting events. This requirement turned sport teams and individual athletes into "representatives" of nations – symbolized through national flags. In contrast to today, however, the IOC did not claim to promote political neutrality at the Olympic Games of the day. Therefore, the use of flags as political symbols was consistent.

Let me introduce you to Baron Charles Pierre de Frédy Coubertin, who was born in the early hours of the year 1863 in Paris. Coubertin is most famous for having established the modern Olympic Games and the foundation of the IOC. His upbringing equipped him with an education at France's most prestigious religious, military, and university institutions. He internalized high society etiquette that served him well when he turned to become a sport administrator in the 1880s. Coubertin was deeply affected by France's defeat in the Franco-Prussian War of 1870/71. Inspired by the English and American use of physical exercise in education, Coubertin regarded sport as the ideal means to improve the fitness of the French youth for potential future military conflicts.[27]

Networker Coubertin is remembered and idolized today to a much larger degree than his contemporaries because he instrumentalized sport *differently*. He took inspiration from the international peace movement, travel and communication expansion, and the world fairs in his successful attempt to establish the Olympic Games to increase peaceful global interaction. Coubertin was, though, more modest than apparent political pacifists such as Czar Nicholas II. He focused on "Olympic internationalism", based on education through sport, but generally shared the same motives as the contemporary peace movement. As such, liberal ideas regarding education, meritocracy, and international cooperation strongly influenced the French Baron.

But we should not mistake Coubertin for a visionary who aimed to reform the global system. As a child of his time, he saw nations as natural and fundamental, rather than something that came about due to historical circumstances or social agreements. Hence, he implemented the nation state concept as a central feature in his Olympic internationalism. For Coubertin, it were the "states and cities" who met at the Olympic Games "in the persons of their young men", not the individual athletes themselves. A gold medal was not an individual's medal but belonged to the nation or state.[28]

Coubertin's attitude is best captured in several of his numerous publications. In 1894, he already showed a contradictory attitude towards international sport: "Internationalism (is) understood, of course, as respect for, not destruction of, native countries. It is a trend that grew out of the deep need for peace and fraternity arising from the depths of the human heart (…)".[29] In his typical excessively fancy prose, he promoted the view that nations are a natural phenomenon.

Thinkers such as Yuval Noah Harari or Benedict Anderson would challenge Coubertin in his assumption that nations are a given. As we have seen, they argue that the emergence of nations has been shaped by social processes and humans imaginative capacities.

Later, in 1907, he addressed the French population to stir their nationalist sentiments:

> Should we abandon France and our flag? Should we no longer be ourselves? (…) No. Love of country has nothing incompatible with our desire for peace. Like our fathers, we want France to be ever more powerful, shining in more glory and beauty, but the times when strength and vitality of nations was showcased above all by cannon fire and saber blows are over.[30]

In his appeal, he demonstrated why he wanted nations to be represented in the Olympic Games. Coubertin wanted to encourage interaction and respect between *nations,* rather than downplaying nationality. For him, the combination of human striving for success and national identity was the magic recipe of the Olympic Games.

It should come as no surprise then that Coubertin sympathized with nationalism. "Nationalism is by no means detrimental," he wrote in 1901. He continued: "National peculiarities are an indispensable prerequisite for the life of a people and that contact with other people will strengthen and enliven them."[31] International sport, Coubertin thought, was the ideal environment to peacefully showcase national characteristics. In his efforts, he lobbied government officials, sport administrators, and aristocrats for years to gain support for his Olympic projects, never shy of highlighting the benefits of participation and success for their – often newly emerging – nations. After all, he also had hoped to strengthen the physicality of French youth for potential future military conflicts with Germany.

Hence, Coubertin set up a system where athletes represent their nations when they compete and participation as individuals was not possible. Only the nations – via their National Olympic Committees (NOCs) could choose athletes to represent them at the Olympic Games. Crucially, this meant that athletes had to wear national uniforms and compete under their national flags – not their sport organization's emblems.

Coubertin was a man of his time and therefore the nation state system was the logical choice when it came to organizing his international sport system. Despite his awareness of the desire of nations to demonstrate their powers on an international stage, he banked on reason and cooperation to prevail. Former US Foreign Minister Henry Kissinger once compared such trust by politicians to the Greek concept of "hybris": a form of spiritual pride that already bore the seed of its own destruction.[32]

We should note, however, that Coubertin was consistent in his approach as far as he did not claim that Olympic sport should be "neutral". The concept of political neutrality is absent from the first editions of the Olympic Charter until after the Second World War. Writing on the eve of the 1936 Berlin Olympic Games, Coubertin showed awareness of the fact that the Olympic idea was not "immune" from national politics.[33] Instead, he focused on peace. It was only after the end of Coubertin's presidency that the IOC demanded from NOC that they must avoid political influence and the Olympic discourse began to highlight that idea the Olympic competitions were contested by individuals and not nations.[34]

Coubertin, always simultaneously diplomat and power broker, was, however, not blind to the danger of nationalist sentiments within the sport system. The institutional legacy of his concerns towards politicization is the IOC itself. He designed the organization as an exclusive group of politically independent individuals, who represented the IOC in their home countries – not the other way around.[35] He did not want IOC members to be representatives of nations (or national federations) within the IOC. This strategic move allowed Coubertin to handpick individuals sympathetic to his cause. Alternative set-ups, for example in governing bodies of individuals sports such as athletics, in which national representatives make the decisions, were vilified by Coubertin as tools of tyranny.[36]

A welcome side-effect for the French Baron was that the resulting early IOC membership mainly comprised of European aristocrats.[37] It was this group of individuals who backed Coubertin's insistence on the inclusion of national flags – even though ironically those symbols in many Western contexts have their origins in *anti*-aristocratic sentiments. Even in 2024, aristocrats like the Princess of Liechtenstein, the Prince of Monaco, the British Princess Royal, the Grand Duke of Luxembourg, the Prince of Jordan, the Prince of Bhutan and the Princess of Saudi-Arabia sit at the IOC's round table.

First signs of failure

It might seem surprising that Coubertin could not enforce his idea to stage the first Olympic Games in his French homeland. Rather, the inaugural members of the IOC chose Athens in 1896 to honor the

Olympics' Ancient roots. The lack of technological developments did not allow for the transmission to the world of moving images from Athens and neither did many newspapers print in color to highlight national flags. However, the flags were a constant presence for those on site. National flag appearance came in threefold manner. First, flags were used to represent nations at the Panathenaic stadium, causing irritation among certain athletes who saw themselves as individuals or club members.[38] Second, the Greek host nation prominently displayed its flag, notably during Spiridon Louis's marathon victory. "Everywhere small Greek flags were waved joyfully by the enthusiastic Greeks," reads the event's official report.[39] Third, national success was symbolized through flags and anthems, with winners' flags hoisted immediately after competitions, emphasizing national recognition over individual achievements, despite medals being awarded only on the last day.[40]

It did not always go according to plan though. Here we return to Alfred Hajós, the Hungarian team captain of the first international football match outside Britain. The multitalented Hajós had been a swimmer prior to his enthusiasm for the round leather ball. In fact, he was tragically tied to water. Hajós was born as Arnold Guttmann in 1878 and had changed his name when his father had drowned in the Danube River: he picked the name Hajós because it meant sailor. Hajós dedicated his early life to survival in the water and became one of seven athletes representing Hungary at the 1896 Olympic Games. He did not lose his sense of humor along the way, however. Legend has it that the King of Greece asked Hajós after his race where he had learned swimming. His answer was: "In the water, Your Majesty".[41] And while the question appears legitimate considering Hungary's lack of access to the sea, Hajós' quick-witted response revealed short-sighted, stereotypical thinking on the King's side.

Hajós and "his" national symbols took center stage after he became the first champion in swimming in Olympic history. Following his victory in the 100-meter freestyle, the orchestra played the Austrian anthem whilst the Hungarian flag was raised.[42] The Austro-Hungarian Empire officially participated as one "nation" at the event, but in practice the two nations' results were listed separately from each other. In fact, the Hungarian flag was only used because a journalist had stolen the flag on departure.[43] In contrast to the decision not to fly any flags at the Austria vs. Hungary game in 1902, the Olympics' desperate fusing of sport with national symbolism already heralded in its natal hours the countless future political conflicts centered around symbolism.

Another incident involving Hajós and his six compatriots is noted in the official report on the Games. It explains in a disapproving tone that the Hungarian Olympic team was too keen on the "self-advertisement" of their national colors because the Hungarians wore their national uniforms even outside the sporting facilities.[44] Maybe Hajós longed for recognition of their nationality since they did not receive it at home prior to their departure. For example, the dean of Hajós' university had only grudgingly permitted him to compete at the Games and did not congratulate him on his return. Hajós was a proud Hungarian and identified much less with his Jewish background – he was, in fact, also the first Jewish athlete to win an Olympic gold medal.[45]

This section started as a history of Pierre de Coubertin, one of the most influential sport officials in the era of modern sport. But it ended with a contextualization of the internationally relatively unknown athlete, Alfred Hajós. Initially, there is no connection between the two, other than their appearance at the first Olympic Games. However, to advance the argument in this book, their link is crucial. It shifts the focus from traditional historical narratives of political leaders, elites, and dominant groups to ordinary people. Specifically, the contrast shows us some of the issues intertwined around the nation concept that Coubertin did not foresee but which are important for us to consider as we imagine alternative traditions at future Olympic Games.

A ceremony around the winner's flag

In the decades after the inaugural Olympic Games in 1896, Coubertin and his contemporaries pushed their belief in the positive effect of national symbols to new extremes. Even though the national flags of the winners had been hoisted after the victories of individual athletes, they had been detached from the medal ceremonies at all Olympic Games between 1896 and 1928. From Athens to Amsterdam, Olympic athletes had received their medals on the final day of the competitions from heads of states. The athletes thereby took an inferior position, walking underneath the balcony/podium on which the dignitaries were located.[46] The power structures were evident.

National flags in sport make it unmistakably obvious that the participating athletes should be regarded as representatives of their countries. The flags are positioned uppermost and made visible to all onlookers. The sport historian John MacAloon sees the positive side of the tradition. He argues that "flags don't rise and an anthem doesn't float down on the champions until after transnational authority has yoked their individual and national bodies with the Olympic medals that transform them into special kinds of human bodies – that is, incorporate them into a status that will thereafter transcend their nationalities and personalities." I, like others, take a different view.[47] Even in the early days of the Olympic movement, sport officials have shown little desire to use sport as a tool to promote peace between nations.[48] Instead, they show realist and conservative attitudes.[49]

A study on the 1932 Olympic Games shows how the media became a powerful ally for the promotion of nationalistic ideas. The US national media coverage of the Games in Los Angeles focused strongly on a competition between nations. "Who won the Olympics?" a writer in the *Los Angeles Times* asked his readers after the event. "The answer comes echoing back from the hills like a clap of thunder. The United States."[50] It was not the athletes who won the medals, but the nation. And how to better symbolize this connection than with the national flag of the most important Olympic winner on the front page? Unsurprisingly, the US flags waved at *Los Angeles Times* readers over the morning coffees.[51] Critical media outlets were largely absent in the United States, and elsewhere in the world, at the time.

Ironically, in the first three editions of the Olympic Games (1896, 1900, and 1904), despite the focus on nations, the organizing committees and the IOC allowed athletes in teams to be of different nationalities.[52] Only with the 1908 Olympic Games was the nation-based structure made mandatory and linked to the existence of a NOC.[53] The IOC later corrected this. However, not by removing the achievements of successful competitors in 1896, 1900, and 1904, but by strengthening the national concept: the IOC retroactively awarded the victories to the winning athletes' nations. In the 1920s, nationality becomes officially included in Olympic regulations as a key criterion for Olympic Games participation.[54]

The focus on national success proved useful for the IOC in the years leading up to the First World War. Nations now began to consider international sport as an arena in which to demonstrate their power.[55] "World opinion" became an issue.[56] For example, no less than three US presidents welcomed the American team after the 1912 Stockholm Olympic Games.[57] The creation of the Olympic Games as an international sporting event required the recognition of common rules, norms, and values by the participating nations. Coubertin thereby created a playing field on which every country could place its national strengths on display. Governments began to promote Olympic medals, as well as success in other sports, as a measurable means to demonstrate a nation's overall power.

As nations' focus on sport grew, Olympic sport administrators decided to display national symbols even more prominently. It all started to change on a cold winter day in the US winter sport resort Lake Placid in early February 1932. The Belgian Count Henri de Baillet-Latour, who had replaced Pierre de Coubertin as IOC President in 1925, had instructed the local organizing committee to create "three pedestals" on which the Olympic medal winners would stand.[58] Fittingly, it was a US athlete who mounted the new podium first, though not on the highest step. Speed skater John Shea, who had won the 500 meters event, received his medal from the hands of Baillet-Latour, standing on the far left side of a rudimentary wooden podium.

Shea was also the second athlete to receive a gold medal on the podium on the next day for his victory in the 1,500 meters, this time standing on top. Miraculously the appearance of the podium had changed though. For the rest of the Games, it was draped in a star-spangled cloth, resembling the US national flag.[59] Every athlete – no matter their citizenship – was now pictured with the US flag. A few months later in Los Angeles, the podium ceremony was then linked with the flag-raising and the playing of the national anthem. Now, *national* success became even more visible. This ritual has been kept to this day.

This decision to combine the flag-raising with the medal ceremony meant that *national* success became even more visible. It was from then on that the national anthem of the nation representing the winner was played and the flag raised to the music. This ritual has been kept until today. Due to the emotionality of the moment, the tradition creates a strong bond between nation, athlete, flag, and spectator.

Conclusion

Knowledge of Coubertin's networking and political lobbying is highly relevant to adopting a critical perspective of the IOC's current stance on political interference in sport. Coubertin's strategic move to tie the Olympic Movement to the nation concept and symbolize the link using national flags had the positive effect that his sport movement received the required support at the beginning of the twentieth century. Since national flags were by far the most widely recognized symbols during Coubertin's age, their inclusion appears logical. Importantly, however, Coubertin did not foresee that the Olympic Games would have to be politically neutral – as is the case today – and therefore he could justify political symbols being included in the Olympic Games.

In contrast, today's sport officials claim that sport and politics should be separated, but continue to rely on political symbols despite the existence of alternatives. For example, NOC or national sport federations all have their own logos today. Take the three English lions, the Korean tiger, the Australian kangaroo, or Uganda's crested crane – these are all internationally known brands. Sure, they also relate to national identity, but they do not symbolize a political entity in the way a national flag does. Other events, like the *Universiade* that features the world's best university athletes, are now also organized around the nation state concept. National university sport federations select the participants, and national flags are used to demarcate the delegations from each other. Even in the field of education the controversial connection between nationhood and the Olympic Movement becomes evident. For example, any individual who wants to participate in certain international education activities of the International Olympic Academy (IOA) can only do so if nominated by an NOC or National Olympic Academy. At the IOA itself, the individuals are then linked symbolically via the national flags to their countries.

In short, the issue of national flags does not seem to arise from Coubertin's original intentions. Rather, the paradox of their use emerges from the contradiction between sports' distancing itself from politics while at the same time relying on political symbols. In the next chapters, I will address this contradiction and its historical emergence in greater depth.

Notes

1 Eric Hobsbawm, *Nations and Nationalism since 1870: Program, Myth, Reality* (Cambridge: Cambridge University Press, 2014), 143.
2 Andrew Heywood, *Global Politics* (London: Palgrave Macmillan, 2011), 64.
3 Greenfeld, *Nationalism*, 22.
4 *Kiøbenhavensposten*, July 11, 1836, accessed via *Mediestream*, http://hdl.handle.net/109.3.1/uuid:97f7d442-69b0-465e-a367-3a218625be21.
5 *Schwäbischer Merkur*, June 4, 1825, accessed via *Deutsches Zeitungsportal*, https://www.deutsche-digitale-bibliothek.de/newspaper.
6 *Staats- und gelehrten Zeitung des Hamburgischen unpartheyischen Correspondenten*, April 13, 1830, accessed via *Deutsches Zeitungsportal*, https://www.deutsche-digitale-bibliothek.de/newspaper.
7 Holger Nehring, "Peace Movements and Internationalism," *Moving the Social* 55 (2016): 93–112.
8 Hidemi Suganami, "A Note on the Origin of the Word 'International'," *British Journal of International Studies* 4, no. 3 (1978): 226–232. 1
9 Nehring, "Peace Movements."
10 *The San Francisco Call*, January 24, 1904, accessed via *Library of Congress*, https://chroniclingamerica.loc.gov/lccn/sn85066387/1904-01-24/ed-1/seq-17/#words=Force+Czar+Nicholas.

11 Kent de Price, "Diary of Nicholas II, 1917–1918, an annotated translation" (Master thesis, University of Montana, 1965).
12 Harman, *A People's History*, 400.
13 Philipp Blom, *The Vertigo Years. Change and Culture in the West, 1900–1914* (New York: Basic Books, 2008), 192–197.
14 Ibid., 196.
15 Bertha von Suttner, "Speech addressed to pacifists in San Francisco – 1912," accessed via *Iowa State University*, https://awpc.cattcenter.iastate.edu/2018/10/17/speech-addressed-to-pacifists-in-san-francisco-1912/.
16 Nehring, "Peace Movements."
17 See for example: Mark Mazower, *Governing the World. The History of an Idea*. (London: Penguin Press, 2012).
18 Richard Hold, *Sport and the British. A Modern History* (Oxford: Clarendon Press, 1989).
19 *North British Daily Mail*, December 2, 1872, accessed via *British Newspaper Archive*, https://britishnewspaperarchive.co.uk/viewer/bl/0002683/18721202/070/0006.
20 John Hoberman, "Toward a Theory of Olympic Internationalism," *Journal of Sport History* 22, no. 1 (1995): 1–37.
21 Ibid.
22 Jason Kaufman and Orlando Patterson, "Cross-National Cultural Diffusion: The Global Spread of Cricket," *American Sociological Review* 70 (2005): 82–110.
23 *Morning Herald (London)*, October 21, 1844, accessed via *British Newspaper Archive*, https://britishnewspaperarchive.co.uk/viewer/bl/0002408/18441021/063/0007.
24 Richard Giulianotti, "Built by the two Varelas: The rise and fall of football culture and national identity in Uruguay," *Sport in Society* 2, no. 3 (1999): 134–154.
25 Interestingly, with football still struggling to gain recognition in many nations with gymnastics traditions where anything English was detested, some players decided to play under pseudonyms to avoid punishments.
26 Karl Lennartz, "The Story of the Rings," *Journal of Olympic History* 10 (2002): 29–61.
27 Pierre de Coubertin, "What we can now ask of sport…", in *Olympism. Selected Writings*, ed. Norbert Müller (Lausanne: International Olympic Committee, 2000), 270.
28 Pierre de Coubertin, "Religio Athletae, " *Bulletin du Bureau International de Pédagogie Sportive* 1 (1928): 5–6.
29 Pierre de Coubertin, "The Neo-Olympism: Appeal to the People of Athens, " in *Olympism. Selected Writings*, ed. Norbert Müller (Lausanne: International Olympic Committee, 2000), 533ff.
30 Pierre de Coubertin, "Pacifisme et nationalisme," *Revue pour les Francais* 2 (April 1907): 603–604.
31 Ramon Spaaj, "Olympic rings of peace? The Olympic movement, peacemaking and intercultural understanding," *Sport in Society* 15, no. 6 (2012): 761–774.
32 Kissinger, *Weltordnung*, 54.
33 Pierre de Coubertin, "Olympism and Politics," in *Olympism. Selected Writings*, ed. Norbert Müller (Lausanne: International Olympic Committee, 2000), 584.

34 Leo Goretti, "Olympic Neutrality and Norm Emergence in International Sport: A Long-Term Perspective," *International Journal of Sport & Society*, in press.
35 Dikaia Chatziefstathiou and Ian P. Henry, *Discourses of Olympism. From the Sorbonne 1894 to London 2012* (London: Palgrave Macmillan, 2012), 24.
36 Letter, Pierre de Coubertin to Godefroy de Blonay, April 20, 1912, Digital Collection "Manuscripts Pierre de Coubertin", A-PO2–1912–04–20, IOC Historical Archives, Lausanne.
37 There were some exceptions, such as Leonard Cuff from New Zealand, Kano Jigoro from Japan, and Angelo Bolanaki from Greece (who also held an Egyptian passport), among others.
38 It is unclear how many nations participated in Athens, however. Most athletes represented clubs and had not been selected by a national sport organization. Even the IOC only lists only fourteen nations but not list which ones.
39 Pierre de Coubertin, Timoleon J. Philemon, N.G. Politis and Charalambos Anninos, *Official Report of the 1896 Olympic Games: Second Part* (Athens: Charles Beck Publisher, 1897), 53.
40 Ibid., 63.
41 Joseph Buchanan, "Hungary's Alfréd Hajós Overcomes Heartbreak to Become First Olympic Champion," *Swimming World*, June 19, 2017, https://www.swimmingworldmagazine.com/news/hungarys-alfred-hajos-overcomes-heartbreak-to-become-first-olympic-champion/#comment-271030.
42 Bill Mallon and Ture Widlund, *The 1896 Olympic Games: Results for All Competitors in All Events, with Commentary* (Jefferson: McFarland & Company), 104.
43 "Alfred Hajos," *Zsidó Kiválóságok Háza Alapítvány*, accessed June 3, 2024, https://www.zsidokivalosagok.hu/en/alfred-hajos/.
44 Geraldine Biddle-Perry, "Clothing the British Olympic Ideal: The Emergence of Olympic Ceremonial Attire, 1896–1924," *Journal of Design History* 25, no. 3 (2012): 252–267.
45 *The Scotsman*, July 8, 1978, accessed via *British Newspaper Archive*, https://britishnewspaperarchive.co.uk/viewer/bl/0000540/19780708/343/0017.
46 Robert K. Barney, "A Simple Souvenir: The Wienecke Commemoration Medal and Olympic Victory Celebration," *Olympika* 15 (2006): 87–110.
47 John Hoberman, "The Myth of Sport as a Peace-Promoting Political Force," *The SAIS Review of International Affairs* 31, no. 1 (2011): 17–29.
48 Ibid.
49 John Hoberman, "Toward a Theory of Olympic Internationalism," *Journal of Sport History* 22, no. 1 (1995): 1–37.
50 Paul Lowry, "America's Supremacy in Athletics Emphatic," *Los Angeles Times*, August 15, 1932, 9, in: Mark Dyreson, "Marketing National Identity: The Olympic Games of 1932 and American Culture," *Olympika* 9 (1995): 23–48.
51 Ibid.
52 John Horne and Garry Whannel, *Understanding the Olympics* (London: Routledge, 2016), 179. Their results are now grouped under the mixed team IOC code ZZX.
53 Jean Loup Chappelet and Brenda Kübler-Mabbot, *The International Olympic Committee and the Olympic System* (London: Routledge, 2008), 51.

54 Trine Nørgaard Pedersen, "The Possibility of Refugee Participation Throughout Olympic History: A Discourse Analysis of the International Olympic Committee's Discursive Construction of the Olympic Games" (Master thesis, Aalborg University, 2020).
55 Robert K. Barney, "The Great Transformation: Olympic Victory Ceremonies and the Medal Podium," *Olympika* 7 (1998): 89–112. 1
56 Keys
57 Barney, "The Great Transformation".
58 Ibid.
59 "Jack Shea," *Olympic.org*, accessed June 6, 2024, https://olympics.com/en/athletes/jack-shea.

3 The Paradox Expanded

> Imagine the chaos in our living room as a small crowd of people made loud and swift political declarations about every country, making the case for why we should cheer or boo. "The Cubans love Palestine," "South Africa is the country of Mandela," "The French gave Israel Mirage fighter jets," "The Americans are biased toward Israel," "The president of this or that country said the Palestinians deserve freedom," "Kenya was occupied by the British too," and so on.[1]

The above observation stems from a Palestinian journalist writing from a Gaza refugee camp. He describes the 2020 Tokyo Olympic Games Opening Ceremony. It is difficult to determine whether the above comments have actually been made. However, having watched different opening ceremonies with people from across the globe, they confirm my impression that political opinions are regularly expressed when national teams march in behind their flags at the Olympic Games. The nations and not the athletes or the sport are in focus.

That said, the parade of nations must be a deeply emotional experience for the participating athletes. Former Zimbabwean swimmer Kirsty Coventry, today an IOC Executive Board member, participated at five Olympic Games. She attended all opening and closing ceremonies: "It's really a special thing."[2] However, reading through her recollections, it is unclear what exactly created her emotions. Coventry speaks about "seeing so many different people" and about looking around and seeing "the scale of everything and then you see the flame – that's when you think 'right, this is it'." Coventry cannot grasp what touched her so deeply at such moments, as we all probably could not. It is evident, however, that her focus was on the

DOI: 10.4324/9781003564058-3

engagement with other individuals and Olympic symbolism. She does not mention her national team or the Zimbabwean flag at all.

Possibly, former Zimbabwean President Robert Mugabe, often called out as tyrant, has a clearer idea. He knows Coventry well. In 2008, Mugabe rewarded Coventry a USD 100,000 cash prize following her four Olympic medals in Beijing. "She is our golden girl", Mugabe argued, indicating that he considered Zimbabwe to have ownership of Coventry. The lines between individual and nation are indeed blurred here. Zimbabwe finished the 2008 Olympic Games as the fourth best African nation. However, it was Coventry alone who secured this result. It is therefore hardly surprising that Mugabe was pleased with Coventry's success. But for what reasons exactly?

We find an answer in Mugabe's attempt to attend the opening ceremony of said Games. In 2008 there were elections in Zimbabwe and Mugabe faced a serious challenge for the presidency, including allegations of irregularities. With the election result in the balance, Mugabe flew to the Beijing Olympic Games in an attempt to demonstrate publicly that he was the rightful president. After all, what better stage than an Olympic opening ceremony where television cameras usually associate a nation's flag with the head of state in the stands. In other words, Mugabe was looking to be linked to the flag – and his golden girl: Coventry was Zimbabwe's flagbearer that year.[3]

Yet, Mugabe had made his plans without the de facto host, the ruling Chinese Communist Party, which controlled all narratives of the Games. China had been a staunch ally of Mugabe during his presidency, publicly considering the relationship between the two countries an "all-weather friendship".[4] However, the storm caused by a potential election loss led China to believe that Mugabe's participation at the opening ceremony would be seen as an affront to his potential successor. Hence, Mugabe's seat in the Beijing Olympic Stadium remained empty as the Chinese authorities denied him entry into the country.[5]

We learn from this episode that the Olympic opening ceremony with the parade of nations appears to be a crucial public opportunity for national governments and powerful individuals to play their political power plays. In 2018, when South Korean and North Korean government officials sat together to watch the opening of the Pyeongchang Winter Olympic Games, the same observation could be made. The inclusion of political symbolism provides the framework for it. The emotions derive from the view taken by athletes, viewers, and politicians of their own flag. This is far from the mixing of cultures that Coubertin's liberalist idea foresaw. Rather, the case outlined seems to confirm realist views of the international sport system. Realist thinkers see rivalry and the pursuit of the national interest dominating over any potential hopes for international cooperation. For realists, internationalism is a utopian delusion.[6]

Over the next pages, I will highlight the way in which IOC's ignorance of political realities, combined with forces far outside of the organization's control, created the perfect storm that continues to disturb international sport today. Through these stories, we see that by sticking with the nation state framework, the Olympics developed into a political arena. They are reflections of the world's political climate, a mirror showing us the power of symbolism and the ongoing tug-of-war between nationalism and global unity.

At the same time, the Olympic powers allowed nations to display flags. Those nations could use the Olympic platform to express a "banal nationalism", a concept introduced by the scholar Michael Billig in the 1990s.[7] Banal nationalism serves the reaffirmation of the nation concept. The flags send messages to a community about who can belong and who must be excluded. And only those who are part of a nation can use the most powerful national symbol: the flag.

Beneficiaries of history's continuation

The novelist George Orwell's poignant observation that "sport is war minus the shooting" dates from 1946.[8] If Orwell had lived beyond 1950, he might have seen sport evolve into a political tool more akin to an atomic bomb than a machine gun. During the Cold War, the Olympic Games were not just about sports; they were a battleground for ideological supremacy, masked by the IOC as a forum for international camaraderie.

The Cold War is also the best thing that happened to the Olympics. It allowed a complete politicization of international sport – represented by the use of national symbols. Through the contest between the Eastern and Western bloc, the Games gained the global popularity it still holds today. Without the Cold War, the Olympic Games would not have the current political and economic status.

True, in 1936 the Nazi regime had already hijacked the Olympic idea by using the event to communicate their claim of Aryan superiority. In the context of Nazi Germany, international sport has proven to be particularly impotent as promoter of peace. Poland, for example, participated in the 1936 Berlin Olympic Games, but the country's involvement did not protect it from the German invasion two years later. During this period, the Olympics failed in its peace-promoting mission.

Symbolism played an important role, too, especially in form of the Nazi flag. In fact, Adolf Hitler had already emphasized the symbolism and color of flags in his book *Mein Kampf.* [9] The flag was a central symbol in the documentaries by Leni Riefenstahl, whose aesthetic formula was based on flags, hymns, and camera movement, which also characterized her other Nazi propaganda films.[10] However, it was only after the Second World War that live broadcasting, color television, and satellite coverage, added more vibrancy and realism to international sport coverage. The IOC played an active role in this development. The three main partners in the Axis alliance of the Second World War all received the right to host Olympic Games during the Cold War: Italy in 1960, Japan in 1964, and Germany in 1972. It was considered a gesture of rehabilitation, but it also allowed the IOC to raise the political interest in hosting the Olympic Games to enhance its movement's global standing. National political interests and political symbols remained important to the IOC. They also contributed to the increasing economic revenues that the Olympic Games produced through the sales of television rights.[11]

What had changed, however, was that the IOC had publicly shifted its stance on the relationship between sport and politics due to the integration of the Soviet Union in the Olympic Movement in the post-war era. The Soviet Union and its allies posed a significant challenge to the IOC because the IOC under the presidency of American Avery Brundage aimed to maintain its monopoly over international sport amidst geopolitical tensions.

The Soviet Union could not be excluded from a movement claiming universality.[12] When the Soviet Union first participated in the 1952 Helsinki Olympic Games, the apparent need to prevent political instrumentalization of the Games became urgent. Brundage, who was a convinced anti-Communist, responded to pro-peace demonstrations by Eastern athletes such as the Czechoslovakian runner Emil Zatopek by introducing regulations to emphasize the non-political nature of the Games.[13] These measures aimed to downplay the political significance of the Games, a necessity for the IOC in the Cold War context, while continuing to profit from the effects of political symbolism. After all, the flags symbolized the political significance of the Games. The IOC's change of direction was more functional than value-based, but sharpened the paradox of the use of flags in Olympic sport.

In the final decade of the Cold War, the superpower rivalry between the United States and the Soviet Union blatantly demonstrated that the Olympics could be co-opted for propaganda purposes. Brundage's successor as IOC President, the Irishman Lord Killanin, once claimed that now "ultra-nationalistic trends" were evident at the Olympic Games.[14] This is best illustrated by taking a closer look at the opening ceremonies of the Olympic Games in 1980 (held in Moscow) and 1984 (held in Los Angeles).

Consider this first scene that took place in Moscow on July 19, 1980, in the Central Lenin Stadium. Five minutes into the Opening Ceremony of the 1980 Olympic Games, the Soviet national anthem rings from the loudspeaker. It is the sign for the spectators on the stands to hold up colored cards. Within seconds, the stadium section opposite the seats of the political guests is transformed into the Soviet coat of arms. Change of cards. Now the Kremlin is depicted.[15] The message was evident: these are the Soviet's Olympic Games. If you want to compete with us, we are ready to fight. The ceremony that was at the time labelled the "most grandiose opening ceremony in Olympic history" presented symbols of Soviet state ideology en masse. Even though many Soviet rivals were absent as they had boycotted the event, they surely watched it on television – and the United States saw itself forced to respond.

Now consider a second scene, this time from the Los Angeles Memorial Coliseum on July 28, 1984. The same message to the attendants as in Moscow: hold up your cards to the sky. This time, the flags of all nations emerged on the stands. Patriotism mixed with world unity were the key message of the Americans. Look world, we are the greatest nation on earth, but we do also value the international community. This time, the Soviets and their allies boycotted the event, but the majority of the symbols in the opening ceremony were meant for them. In January, they had announced they would station nuclear bombs in East Germany, and at the time of the opening ceremony, they were running their largest military offensive in Afghanistan. On the penultimate day of the Games, US President Ronald Reagan joined in the symbolic messages. He started a radio voice check with the words: "My fellow Americans. I'm pleased to tell you today that I've signed legislation that will outlaw Russia forever. We begin bombing in five minutes."[16] He later apologized for the "joke".

It played into the hosts' script that the most successful athlete at the 1984 Games was the American four-time gold medal winner Carl Lewis. And Lewis added yet another dimension to the association between national flags and success to Olympic history. Following his victory in the 100-meters competition, he ran a lap of honor with the US flag on his shoulders. Lewis argued that his extra lap was a spontaneous emotional reaction, though the media speculated that the extra minutes of America's best athlete wrapped in the national flag was a scene directed from above. Staged or not, it was the start of yet another flag-promoting ritual.[17] The lap of honor in the athletics stadium is today a custom regularly exercised by athletes. For them, it is an extended time with public attention. But it is unlikely that they realize how they let themselves be instrumentalized by carrying a national flag with them.

The face-off between the United States and the Soviet Union is often believed to have nearly destroyed international sport. It did, however, save the Olympic idea. The symbolic significance political entities attributed to the Olympic Games gave those in the Olympic Movement their confidence back. Cities showed renewed interest in staging the Olympics.[18] Potential future hosts realized that national symbolism at the Games was a hugely effective way to communicate national identity.

Certainly, the development of the television medium served as a blessing for the IOC and the Cold War superpowers. Anyone seeking to popularize their cause could receive global attention by promoting their views at the Olympic Games. Flags and other political symbols could now be seen in color and in real time. Viewers could easily take sides, and a flying flag at the Olympic Games meant national pride and global status for governments. The IOC then began to understand the economic potential of tying its internationalist idea to political symbols. Throughout the 1980s, it set up its global sponsorship program and began to sell the Olympic symbols to commercial partners. Those, too, utilized national identity to sell their products. "When the U.S. wins, you win," claimed McDonalds, for example, in one of its advertisements around the 1984 Games.

Let us consider a last scene, this time from Berlin's Brandenburg Gate on the evening of November 9, 1989. The fall of the Berlin Wall de facto ended the Cold War confrontation. I watched the scenes in my South German home. It was a deeply emotional experience for my family: my grandmother had escaped from East Germany shortly before the construction of the wall. Whilst many in the IOC must have been less positively affected of the historical event, they also had less to worry about. The Cold War had resulted in the Olympic Movement gaining significance and a future-orientated economic structure.

Francis Fukuyama saw in the fall of the Berlin Wall "the end of history".[19] He interpreted the event as the triumph of liberal democracy over Communism. Fukuyama predicted that nationalism would not disappear but that liberal principles would control it. The current geopolitical climate reveals that Fukuyama was mistaken. Russia's invasion in Ukraine. The Gaza conflict. Israel's shooting war with Iran. North Korea's ballistic missiles. It is fair to say that nationalism, violent conflicts, and exclusion continue to characterize the international arena. We appear to be further away from easy resolutions than in the early 1990s.

In this section, we have learned how the Olympic Movement came to provide nations in conflict (and their more peaceful counterparts) with a global platform on which to demonstrate their nationalism. Here, political powerholders find an opportunity to reaffirm national identities, often centered around political leadership. Mugabe's desperate attempt to attend the 2008 Olympic Games opening ceremony illustrates this perfectly. Political leaders also find in the Olympic Games like-minded individuals through whom they will find reassurance for their own beliefs. Since the IOC benefits financially from the inclusion of political actors, symbolized through national flags, there seems to be little motivation to do away with the symbols despite them contradicting the liberalism that lies behind the Olympic idea. The IOC must applaud the continuation of history.

Footballers of the revolution

Another global development reaffirmed the national principles and flags in Olympic sport, namely the decolonialization process. Nations emancipated themselves from their existing ordering powers as they strove for independence. In Asia, the majority of nations accepted the principles of the Peace of Westphalia. The nation state became the main unit in organizing national and international affairs. On the African continent and in the Middle East, the process was less linear and often included military conflicts, revolts, or years of war.[20]

The new nation states sought out sport as the platform to visibly declare independence. It was here that they could show their national flags. The scholars Ian Henry and Mansour Al-Tauqi counted the number of new nations recognized by the IOC for each decade of the twentieth century.[21] They show that in the 1960s the number peaked at 28 new NOCs, of which 22 came from Africa alone. In the same decade, the United Nations recognized 27 new members.[22] Not many of the new nations had instant success. Mugabe's Zimbabwe had. At the nation's first Olympic Games in Moscow in 1980, the Zimbabwean women's hockey team upset its rivals and won the gold medal. The unexpected victory was not just a sporting triumph but also a declaration of Zimbabwe's national identity; an identity crafted under the shadow of colonial rule. Mugabe happily moved his nation into the nation-system at the Olympics to maintain power and bask in the global limelight as he continued to do throughout his regime.

As I thought about this issue, I was reminded about a cartoon in which three athletes representing Japan, China and the Philippines are starting a race, each with the flag of their nation behind them and emblazoned on their singlet.[23] The Japanese and Chinese athletes have only one flag. Behind the Filipino athlete, there are two: the American flag and the Philippines' flag. Moreover, the angle of the Filipino athlete's body in the cartoon makes it impossible to decipher which flag is on his singlet. Whether he is Filipino or American is left for the reader to decide. The cartoon illustrates the 1925 Far Eastern Championships for which the United States as colonizers approved the use of the Philippines' flag in the host city of Manila. Filipino athletes could compete under the flag of the Philippines, but the Americans insisted that the event would take place under the American flag in the presence of US sport officials.[24] Such insistence on US national symbolism served to underscore the status of the Philippines as a colonized nation. In short, the cartoon gives us a first indication that the representation of one nation or flag might not be so straightforward after all.

A similar tension between colonizer and suppressed occurred more than three decades later between Algeria and France. Here, the Algerian athletes, football players in this case, took their destiny in their own hands.

Algeria was amongst the first African nations to realize the role of sport in internationalizing the country's fight against colonialization.[25] Football, for which Algerians always had a strong passion and was also the most popular sport in their colonial overlord, France, was an obvious choice. Internally, the Algerian Liberation Front (FLN), the principle nationalist movement during Algeria's quest for independence, considered football an ideal means to foster national unity. Externally, football was used as a diplomatic tool – all nations that competed against an independent Algerian team essentially recognized the country.

In 1958, the FLN created a national revolutionary team and ordered all Algerian football players, who mainly played for French clubs, to join the new team. The impact was instant. International newspapers reported already weeks prior to the new team's first match on "Patriots to Form 'Free Algerian' Football Eleven".[26] The announcement already had the desired effect even without a ball having been kicked by any of the now Algerian players.

Answering the call was not without risk for individual players. According to FIFA regulations at the time, a professional player could not join another club or play for a national team without the authorization of their current club.[27] Since Algeria's most skilled players were all contracted in France, this rule became suddenly very political. The fact that those prominent players signed up despite such potential consequences shows their commitment to the Algerian cause. Amongst those who answered to the call was Rachid Mekhloufi, one of the most skillful players in France and at the time a certain selection for France's 1958 World Cup squad. Clearly, Mekhloufi prioritized the political cause over his sporting prospects.

From an Algerian perspective, the initiative was a resounding success, and not only because prominent players signed up. Between 1958 and 1961, the team played against a host of allied nations such as the Soviet Union, China, and numerous Arab countries.[28] In addition, the team adopted a uniquely attractive and fluid offensive playing style with which Algerians could identify.[29] Observers later considered the team as an embodiment of the liberation movement's momentum towards victory.[30] The – by then not official – Algerian flag played a central role in demonstrating Algeria's independence to foreign audiences. The team also wore the colors of the Algerian flag. In Algeria itself, the flag was raised in towns where hundreds gathered to listen to radio broadcasts of the games. Eleven footballers became a national symbol, and only that. FIFA, under influence from France, did not recognize an Algerian national team until the nation's independence in 1962.

Precisely sixty years later, French players with Algerian roots have not forgotten the independence movement and the role football played therein. In 2022, Karim Benzema – who had won the 2018 FIFA World Cup with France – dedicated his Balon d'Or title for the best individual football player to "the people". In doing so, he was referring to the Algerian liberation's main credo: "Only one hero – the people".[31] While officially representing France, Benzema continued to identify with the nation of his ancestors. Here we see that identity goes far beyond the nation a player might represent on the sporting field.

The journey of nations such as Algeria to the fields of international sports are clearly a testament to their citizens resilience and desire to assert their identity on their terms. They quickly bought into international sport because it provided them with an opportunity to announce their independence globally via their national symbols. Since the Olympic Movement in the post-War period only disassociated itself from politics on paper, while continuing to embrace individual nations, it provided the perfect framework for new nations to engage with the established powers. Sport reflects the broader socio-political battles these nations continue to fight. As we will see later, for individual athletes, such as Benzema or Mekhloufi, the matter was and is much more complex. As these countries navigate their post-colonial realities, the interplay between national identity, cultural heritage, and the globalized concept of the nation state remains a critical field of discourse and contestation.

Flags of all committees

The two examples of the Cold War powers and the decolonialization process show us how the Olympic system continued to be exploited for political purposes. In the next step, I will highlight how increasing geopolitical complexity made it very challenging for the IOC to uphold the newly defined principles of political neutrality.

Imagine a sports world where China voluntarily sat out the Olympic Games. This seems an unthinkable scenario today, considering China's powerful role in sport politics in recent Olympics, including hosting the event in 2008 and 2022. These Olympics were not merely sport competitions, but they allowed China stages to broadcast as a global political and economic powerhouse. Yet, if we rewind to a few decades ago, we will find a different story, in which China chose to remain an outsider to the Olympic Movement until 1984, following its own set of rules rather than conforming to the international playbook.

The Chinese Civil War in the late 1940s between nationalists and Communists provided the political backdrop for the episode. In December 1949, the nationalists moved the capital of "their" Republic of China to Taiwan and established a new capital in Taipei.[32] In the meantime, Mao Zedong and the Chinese Communist party took control on the mainland and founded the People's Republic of China. The problem for sport lay in the fact that each side refused to maintain diplomatic relations with nations that officially recognized the other side. It did not take long for questions to arise over who would represent "China" at the Olympic Games. And which flag was to be used as political signifier.

Both Chinas sent teams to compete at the 1952 Olympic Games. Taiwan eventually refused to compete due to the invitation extended to the Communists. There was a delay in the arrival of the Chinese delegation, allowing only for one athlete to compete at the Games. Four years later, the Communist Chinese opted to boycott the Olympics, refusing to budge unless the IOC banned Taiwan from competing. The Taiwanese did travel to Melbourne, however, and were confronted with an unpleasant surprise: the flag raised to represent them was the flag of Communist China.[33] This mishap would be the last time that the Communist flag flew at the Olympic Games for nearly three decades, as the People's Republic boycotted the event due to the IOC's recognition of Taiwan as an independent – Chinese – nation.

The China question over the name and flag used by Taiwan resurfaced in 1976. Prior to the Olympic Games in Moscow, the Canadian government decided not to allow Taiwan to use its name, anthem or flag at the event because it did not want to acknowledge that Taiwan represented the sole legal government in China. Several compromises were offered to the Taiwanese. One of the options was to march behind the Olympic flag and use the Olympic anthem. Taiwanese sport officials rejected this possibility outright as a form of discrimination and offered the IOC a different proposal: all the teams at the Olympics should simply use the Olympic flag.[34] Now it was the IOC's turn to reject an idea on the spot. Taiwan's suggestion, however, would communicate an important message: all nations should be treated the same irrespectively of their international recognition, a suggestion much closer to the IOC's policy of political neutrality.

IOC members pondered for many hours over a solution to the problem in the days leading up to the Montreal Games. Some of the more cynical IOC members wanted the IOC to fly the Taiwanese national flag for two athletes that had already been admitted, and "see the reaction of the [Canadian] Government on the spot."[35] While this idea did not pass muster, the problem remained. The eventual resolution passed by the IOC was to suspend the IOC rule that every team in the Opening Ceremony had to have a placard inscribed with the name of the area or the country.[36] This ruling would have allowed the ROC to compete as "Taiwan" and use its own flag and anthem. The ROC refused and boycotted.[37]

At the end of the 1970s, China had changed its foreign political strategy. Following Mao Zedong's death in 1976, China pushed for reform and began to play by the rules of the international community. Notably, China entered international organizations and pushed for participation in the Olympic Games. The Chinese demanded that the international community adjusted some of its regulations in return, however. In the IOC, this included once again a removal of any political symbolism related to Taiwan. In other words, China pushed the IOC to depart from its use of national symbolism. The IOC backed down. In a 1979 resolution the IOC got Taiwan to consent to participating in international sport under the condition that it was referred to as “Chinese Taipei”. The NOC’s anthem, flag, and constitutions were adopted accordingly. Until today, Taiwan’s political flag is absent from the Games and a specially designed NOC flag is used at the Games. The IOC – contrary to its general principles – did have the power to make concessions to its rules. In fact, the IOC amended several rules of the Olympic Charter in conjunction with the Taiwan decision, allowing in principle all NOCs to be able to opt for their NOC instead of their national flag.[38] Many NOCs already used the new flexibility at that year’s Summer Games in Moscow to protest against the Soviet Union’s invasion of Afghanistan. A crucial difference for Taiwan, however, remains in place. Its NOC does not have the option to participate under its national flag. This decision was further reinforced throughout the 1980s and 1990s by the policies of the Olympic Council of Asia strongly influenced by mainland China.[39]

The Olympic history of the two Chinas illustrates that the IOC made concessions to its rules over time according to where the majority of political sympathies lay. In the 1980s, a crisis-struck IOC was desperate to get the People’s Republic into the Olympics, as the inclusion of China promised political relevance and commercial benefits. The change in attitude did, however, further contradict the IOC’s continued focus on national symbolism, as there is now a nation that cannot participate under its national flag.

China’s self-imposed Olympic quarantine and the eventual resolution of the “two Chinas” problem has a twofold implication. One the one hand, it vividly illustrates how IOC is ostensibly committed to the Peace of Westphalia nation state system. One the other hand, it then highlights how the IOC displayed remarkable flexibility when pressed by geopolitical necessities. Allowing Taiwan to compete as “Chinese Taipei” contradicts the IOC’s nominal policy of strict nation state representation, revealing an adaptability that might not be readily apparent given its historical rigidity. This contradiction is not just a minor footnote; it highlights a broader tension within the IOC’s operations that we will continue to explore in this chapter. While the organization has historically pushed for a rigid application of the nation state model, the practical realities of international relations and the unique political situations of member countries have sometimes forced it to bend its own rules without departing from its principles completely.

Sport as tool of politics

Changes to global political orders through the breakdown of regimes also challenged the static nation system in the Olympic Movement. In such instances, national politics and world events dictated participation in the Olympic Games and the use of national flags. This is despite the fact that the current IOC President, Thomas Bach, could argue, against the backdrop of the participation of Russian and Belarussian athletes at the 2024 Olympic Games: "If politics can decide who take part of the competition, the sport and athletes become tool of politics".[40] There are plenty of examples that contradict Bach's statement. Here, I will, focus on a relatively under-reported case where several nations appeared as part of different teams under their Olympic flags.

At the final of the basketball event at the 1988 Seoul Olympic Games, the flags of Yugoslavia and the USSR were hoisted. The Soviets had beaten the Yugoslavs and had never been in danger throughout the match. Four years later, neither the Yugoslavian nor the Soviet flag flew at the Olympics. Both states had broken up. The IOC allowed individual Yugoslavian athletes – but not teams – to participate as "independent Olympic participants" at the Games because Yugoslavia had embarked on the Balkan war a few weeks earlier. In addition, athletes from twelve former Soviet states made up a "Unified Team". The "independent Olympic athletes" were not allowed to participate in the opening ceremony but were given the Olympic flag during competition. The "Unified Team" marched behind the Olympic flag in the opening ceremony, but when a team member won a medal, the national flag of the medalist's nation was raised. In team events, the IOC decided that the "Unified Team" had to use the Olympic flag and the Olympic hymn.

Any entanglement of this complicated situation must begin with a distinction between timelines. The IOC had almost two years to react to the dissolution of the Soviet Union. IOC officials could sit down with politicians and sport officials to find a solution. The Kremlin, surely a highly political and potentially intimidating location, provided the setting for the most important meeting. The Russian President Boris Yeltsin had issued the invitation, and since the IOC now had an ever-stronger commercial interest to maintain Russia in the Olympics, IOC administrators attended in numbers.[41] From the meeting's minutes, it becomes clear that Yeltsin drove a double-edged strategy. For 1992, he wanted to demonstrate that Russia still considered it had hegemony over the newly independent nations. Therefore, he was in favor of using the Olympic flag "to keep what could still be maintained together".[42] The IOC fulfilled his wish since the recognition of the former Soviet republics NOCs outside the Baltic states had not yet been solved: a "Unified Team" of former Soviet republics was entered for the 1992 Olympic Games in Barcelona. In taking this position, the IOC followed the initial political position taken by the then US President George Bush after the Soviet Union's breakup. In a speech in Kiev in the summer of 1991, Bush had warned Ukraine like other former Soviet republics, to renounce from "suicidal nationalism" for fear of military conflicts. He saw in Russia a valuable future partner and supported the Russian push for a Russian confederation. Bush's position only changed a few months later when the Ukrainian parliament voted for independence and the White House supported that decision.[43]

Yeltsin did, however, also demand that the IOC step up what he called "personalization" of the new NOCs, including Russia. After all, the Russians wanted to return to being the sporting power that the Soviet Union had been. Like the "Unified Team", the IOC granted his wish: four days after the Olympic fire was extinguished, the Russian NOC was recognized. The IOC could not afford to lose a sporting superpower again; the Russian flag had to fly at the Games to highlight its political relevance.

In stark contrast, the recognition of Ukraine and other former Soviet NOCs was delayed until 1993. It became clear that the issue of Russia was more important, with Russian sport enjoying greater status within the IOC. This is also evident at the first Olympics in 1994, when both the Ukraine and Russia participated. One Ukrainian athlete won a gold medal: 16-year-old Oksana Baiul marginally beat the American Nancy Kerrigan in the figure skating final. However, the Norwegian organizers had a problem: they did not have a tape with the Ukrainian anthem. With apparently little political sensitivity, Norwegian officials offered instead to play the old Soviet anthem! After twenty minutes, a Ukrainian sport administrator could eventually step in and provide a tape.[44] This issue did not occur for the Russian athletes, who came home with the largest number of gold medals. The Games marked a new era of Russian political power demonstration via sport. That development culminated twenty years later in the staging of the 2014 Sochi Olympic Games, which were full of political symbolism, and with the subsequent invasion of Crimea a few weeks later.[45]

As for the case of Yugoslavia, the IOC had no time to accept any invitations to Belgrade, nor had the nation played a crucial role in Olympic history – despite its basketball success. The IOC's hands were tied, too. The United Nations had adopted a resolution in May 1992 that would lead to an embargo in international engagement with Yugoslavia. It was for the Spanish government to decide whether any athletes holding Yugoslavian passports could enter the country to compete in the 1992 Barcelona Olympic Games. The resolution forced the IOC to engage with governments on their positions. It emerged quickly that the United Nations, as well as most Western governments, were in favor of letting individual Yugoslavian athletes compete "as private individuals".[46] Any possible identification of Yugoslavians as a team was strongly rejected and, even though one Yugoslavian sport official is quoted as saying: "rather than be present with no name, no country, no flag, we will not come," a few Yugoslavians started as "independent Olympic athletes".

Such an example of an evolving global political landscape shows how the IOC repeatedly finds itself at the intersection of sport and international relations, due to its reliance on national symbolism. The dissolution of the Soviet Union and Yugoslavia embroiled the IOC in the complexities of political change. This makes a balancing of the ideal of neutrality in sports with the realities of geopolitical shifts almost impossible. The case of the "Unified Team" or the ad hoc arrangements for athletes from the former Yugoslavia in 1992, are illustrative of how the IOC's century-old frameworks appear ill-equipped to adapt to dynamic changes.

Conclusion

At the time of the Olympic Movement's foundation, the international system was still relatively stable. Hence, Coubertin mirrored the global order around nations in his establishment of the Olympic Games. However, over the course of a century, we have seen that rival ambitions between nations have deeply impacted the international order and with it the global sport system. New power structures, processes and identities have emerged from globalization. We have also seen that nations continue to work towards their own advantage rather than striving for global harmony.

It would be unfair to Coubertin to put the blame for the controversies his ideologies caused after his lifetime on him. Like any other individual, he was deeply affected by the societal and political circumstances during which he lived. I am having a harder time absolving his successors. Some of the blame for the continuing paradox lies squarely at their feet. The continual insistence that the Olympic Games does not delve into political issues did not help matters but rather made the IOC seem completely out of touch with reality.

In doing so, the Olympic Movement continues to provide nations with a platform to demonstrate difference, strength, and conflict – symbolized through their flags. The logic of the nation and its flags are and always have been increasingly problematic for sport as they impinge on sport's neutral, internationalist objectives. The flags, literally, symbolize the fact that international sporting events such as the Olympic Games are not an apolitical space. They expose the limits of determining what falls within the realm of politics as nations continue to strive for global recognition. But how much tension can the IOC sustain? How long can it cling to its original framework and reject the increasing diversity of political units?

The IOC also demands an organizational framework based on nations and with the inclusion of national flags from any new sport, whose organizers are then confronted with the same political challenges. We can take esports as an example. Esports, or competitive video gaming, present a revolutionary model in the world of sports, one that is largely detached from national identities and borders. This global nature allows players from anywhere to compete in an atmosphere that values skill and community over nationality. However, the IOC insists on traditional nation state structures for integrating esports, requiring a governing body linked to national federations. The International Esports Federation (IESF) has claimed to be such an organization but in 2022, following Russia's invasion of Ukraine, saw itself forced to act due to its structure and expelled its Russian member federation. This decision reflected the influence of national politics on international sports bodies. However, by summer 2023, the IESF had become one of the first international federations to allow Russian players to use national flags again.[47] This decision was influenced by the Romanian-American IESF President who also held the position as General Director of the International Judo Federation – the first Olympic sport federation that allowed Russian and Belarussian athletes to compete in world championships as neutrals in 2023.[48] Once he was voted out of his IESF presidency, the federation reverted its decision.[49]

This flip-flop decision-making underscores how national politics can seep into even the most globally minded sports communities such as esports. Where esports are played outside Olympic settings, they offer an alternative format based on inclusivity and global engagement rather than national representation. Yet, as they moves closer to Olympic inclusion, they face the same old challenges. The necessity for a governing body with national federations, as demanded by the IOC, forces esports into the same framework that has historically amplified nationalistic tensions in sports. Esports should be warned that if it enters an outdated system that prioritizes national symbolism over global connections, it will face the same balancing act between sport and politics.

Notes

1 Ramzy Baroud, "Palestinians' Cheers And Jeers At The Olympics – OpEd," *eurasiareview*, August 3, 2021, https://www.eurasiareview.com/03082021-palestinians-cheers-and-jeers-at-the-olympics-oped/.
2 "Kirsty Coventry: 'I refused to miss the opening and closing ceremonies'," *Olympic.org*, accessed June 6, 2024, https://olympics.com/en/news/kirsty-coventry-i-refused-to-miss-the-opening-and-closing-ceremonies.
3 "Mugabe 'told to stay away' from Games opening," *Mail & Guardian*, August 5, 2008, https://mg.co.za/article/2008-08-05-mugabe-told-to-stay-away-from-games-opening/.
4 "An all-weather friend in Africa," *The Business Report*, n.d., http://www.the-businessreport.com/article/china-and-zimbabwe-celebrate-35th-anniversary-of-diplomatic-ties/.
5 "Beijing Bids Goodbye to Robert Mugabe", New York Times Magazine, December 19, 2017, https://www.nytimes.com/2017/12/19/magazine/beijing-bids-goodbye-to-robert-mugabe.html.
6 Heywood, *Global Politics*, 55ff.
7 Michael Billig, *Banal Nationalism* (London: Sage, 1995).
8 "The Sporting Spirit," *The Orwell Foundation*, accessed 7 June 2014, https://www.orwellfoundation.com/the-orwell-foundation/orwell/essays-and-other-works/the-sporting-spirit/.
9 Adolf Hitler, *Mein Kampf* (Boston: Houghton Mifflin, 1999).
10 Michael Mackenzie, "From Athens to Berlin: The 1936 Olympics and Leni Riefenstahl's Olympia," *Critical Inquiry* 29, no. 2 (2003): 302–36
11 Stephen R. Wenn and Robert K. Barney, *The Gold in the Rings* (Champaign: University of Illinois Press, 2020).
12 Barbara Keys, "The Early Cold War Olympics, 1952–1960: Political, Economic and Human Rights Dimensions," in *The Palgrave Handbook of Olympic Studies*, eds. Helen Jefferson Lenskyj and Stephen Wagg, (London: Palgrave MacMillan, 2012), 72–87.
13 Leo Goretti, "Olympic Neutrality and Norm Emergence in International Sport: A Long-Term Perspective," The International Journal of Sport and Society, in press.
14 "KILLANIN ASSUMES TOP OLYMPIC POST," *New York Times*, September 13, 1979, https://www.nytimes.com/1972/09/13/archives/killanin-assumes-top-olympic-post-irish-lord-receives-keys-in.html.
15 Philip Barker, "Philip Barker: Moscow – the best and most political Olympic Opening Ceremony," *insidethegames*, May 28, 2020, https://www.insidethegames.biz/articles/1094709/blog-moscow-1980-olympics.
16 "President's Joke About Bombing Leaves Press in Europe Unamused," *New York Times*, August 14, 1984, https://www.nytimes.com/1984/08/14/world/president-s-joke-about-bombing-leaves-press-in-europe-unamused.html.
17 Klaus Zeyringer, *Olympische Spiele. Eine Kulturgeschichte von 1896 bis heute: Band 1: Sommer* (Berlin: S. Fischer, 2016), 543.
18 Philip Barker, "The Hidden Legacies of Moscow '80: Changes in Ceremonial and Attitudes," *Journal of Olympic History* 18, no. 2 (2010): 32–37.
19 Francis Fukuyama, *The End of History and the Last Man* (New York: Free Press, 1992).
20 Kissinger, *Weltordnung*, 202.

21 Ian Henry and Mansour Al-Tauqi, "The Development of Olympic Solidarity: West and Non-West (Core and Periphery) Relations in the Olympic World," *The International Journal of the History of Sport* 25, no. 3 (2008): 355–369.

22 "Growth in United Nations membership," *United Nations*, accessed June 9, 2024, https://www.un.org/en/about-us/growth-in-un-membership.

23 Stefan Hübner, "Images of the Sporting 'Civilizing Mission': The Far Eastern Championship Games (1913–1934) and Visions of Modernization in English-Language Philippine Newspapers," *Journal of World History* 27, no. 3 (2016): 497–533.

24 Minutes, 1924 Session of the International Olympic Committee in Paris, June 25 – July 12, 1924, Digital Collection "IOC Session Minutes", IOC Historical Archives, Lausanne, 6.

25 Mahfoud Amara and Ian Henry, "Between globalization and local 'Modernity': The diffusion and modernization of football in Algeria," *Soccer & Society* 5, no. 1 (2004): 1–26.

26 *Civil & Military Gazette (Lahore)*, April 18, 1958, accessed via *British Newspaper Archive*, https://britishnewspaperarchive.co.uk/viewer/bl/0003221/19580418/138/0013.

27 *Civil & Military Gazette (Lahore)*, April 21, 1958, accessed via *British Newspaper Archive*, https://britishnewspaperarchive.co.uk/viewer/bl/0003221/19580421/163/0015.

28 Amara and Henry, "Between globalization and local 'Modernity'."

29 Peter Alegi, *How a Continent Changed the World's Game* (Ohio: Ohio University Press, 2010), 48.

30 Stanislas Frenkiel, "The Nationalization of Algerian Football Following Independence, 1962–1982," *The International Journal of the History of Sport* 38, no. 9 (2021): 972–87.

31 Sami Everett, "Algeria and France: Historical & Experiential Layers of a Footballing Relationship," *Asian Journal of Sport History & Culture* 1, no. 3 (2022): 250–70.

32 I will use Taiwan when referring to the Republic of China for matters of clarity

33 Minutes, Meeting of the IOC Executive Board in Melbourne, November 17, 1956, Digital Collection "IOC Executive Board Minutes", IOC Historical Archives, Lausanne, 1.

34 Minutes, 1976 Session of the International Olympic Committee in Montreal, July 13–19, 1976, Digital Collection "IOC Session Minutes", IOC Historical Archives, Lausanne, 9.

35 Minutes, 1976 Session of the International Olympic Committee, 15.

36 Ibid.

37 Ibid., 18–19 and 69.

38 Modifications to the Olympic Charter accepted in: Minutes, 1980 Session of the International Olympic Committee in Lake Placid, February 10–13, 1980, Digital Collection "IOC Session Minutes", IOC Historical Archives, Lausanne, 9.

39 Jörg Krieger, "The foundation and early years of the Olympic Council of Asia," in *The Routledge Handbook of Sport in Asia*, eds. Fan Hong and Lu Zhouxiang (London: Routledge, 2020): 107–117.

40 Nadine Schmidt and Sammy Mncwabe, "IOC President Thomas Bach defends plan to include Russian and Belarusian athletes at Paris

Olympics," *CNN*, March 23, 2023, https://edition.cnn.com/2023/03/23/sport/thomas-bach-paris-olympics-russia-ukraine-intl-spt/index.html.

41 Minutes, 1992 Session of the International Olympic Committee in Barcelona, July 21–23, 1992, Digital Collection "IOC Session Minutes", IOC Historical Archives, Lausanne, 6–11.

42 Ibid.

43 Serhii Plokov, *The Gates of Europe. A History of Europe* (London: Penguin Books, 2015), 318.

44 "Cool Runnings. Exhausted Lillehammer Officials Proud of 'Norwegian Way' Festival," *The Washington Post*, February 27, 1994, https://www.washingtonpost.com/archive/sports/1994/02/28/cool-runnings/27515c96-d1c7-482a-b1d3-e1b7cad32a91/.

45 Jonathan Grix and Nina Kramareva, "The Sochi Winter Olympics and Russia's Unique Soft Power Strategy," *Sport in Society* 20, no. 4 (2015): 461–75.

46 Minutes, 1992 Session of the International Olympic Committee in Barcelona, 6–11.

47 "Facts regarding OGM 2023 decision and Russian / Ukrainian Participation," *World Esports*, September 2, 2023, https://iesf.org/ogm2023/.

48 "Esport to allow Russian competitors to fly national flag," *Sportstar*, August 29, 2023, https://sportstar.thehindu.com/other-sports/russia-esports-team-to-take-part-in-competitions-under-its-own-flag-international-esport-federation/article67247502.ece.

49 "Board's Decision Regarding Ukraine NF Complaint," *World Esports*, January 18, 2024, https://iesf.org/boards-decision/.

4 The Human Factor

I find the concept of "liquid modernity" useful for an understanding of the state of our present-day societies. Zygmunt Bauman introduced the concept to explain how global communities have departed from stable structures, institutions, and identities. Bauman argues that today we face changes, fragmentation and individualization in our lives.[1] This also applies to the nation state system, which Bauman sees as eroding. States are losing control over their populations and power has been increasingly privatized.

In the previous chapter, we have seen that this development also challenged the international sport system. I will advance this argument over the next pages by switching focus to the role of individuals within the process. Bauman's liquid modernity serves me well here because individuals have multiple, overlapping identities. I touched on this already in the case of Karim Benzema. Moreover, digital technologies and the global economy allow individuals to mobilize collective action or switch allegiances quickly. Citizens become disconnected from representation through a nation.

If true, Bauman's observations are detrimental to the Olympic world. It would mean that individuals' identities will not center around national belonging for much longer. Rather, multi-culturalism, hybrid identities and migration will present an even greater challenge to a sport system based around the nation.[2] In the question of the participation of Russian and Belarussian athletes at the 2024 Olympic Games, the IOC essentially acknowledged the significance of individual identities. The IOC ruled that only athletes, who had no association with the military or who voiced no public support for the war qualified for the AIN team.[3]

Critics might argue that athletes who abandon their national identity are driven by economic or individual political interests. However, in this section, I aim to demonstrate that for more than a century

DOI: 10.4324/9781003564058-4

athletes have rejected or embraced flags other than the one that was meant to represent them in international sport. Individual athletes have always displayed a more fluid and unrestricted sense of identity. Some athletes were forced to compete under several national symbols, others chose to do so. We will see that flags exist in a field of conflict about whether the groups they symbolize have the right to be represented in the spaces they have entered. The sociologist Joost Jansen highlights a key issue here by asking the question, "Who 'genuinely' belongs to the community and should be eligible to wear its vest, *wave its flag (emphasis added)* and sing its hymn during the greatest mediatized sporting event on the planet?"[4] I shall now seek to explore the complexity of this question by focusing on the athletes' perspective.

"I ran for myself"

The IOC's controversial policies to resolve disputes regarding national representation at the Olympics already appeared at early versions of the event. The Finnish-born distance runner Hannes Kolehmainen won gold medals for Finland at the 1912 and 1920 Olympic Games. His home nation had, however, been a Grand Duchy of Russia since 1809. With Coubertin's blessing, Finland was allowed to compete at the Olympic Games in 1908 and 1912. Finland's results were separate from those of Russia, but the Finns had to fly the Russian flag.

Problems began to emerge once the Finnish athletes started excelling in competitions. Enter Kolehmainen. The runner won three gold medals in the 5,000 meter, 10,000 meter, and marathon races at the 1912 Stockholm Olympic Games. Following his victory in the 5,000, Kolehmainen allegedly pointed at the Russian flag and stated, "I would almost rather not have won, than see that flag up there."[5] The story is anecdotal and came from an athlete who was there in Stockholm and reported it at the time. Aside from this one incident, there is scant evidence of Kolehmainen adopting further political positions against Russia, probably because Russia's control over Finland ended with the abdication of Czar Nicholas II and Finland's declaration of independence in 1917.

There is even more evidence in my next example. American citizens picking up the *New York Times* in August of 1936 would have seen the front-page headline about a Japanese marathon runner at the 1936 Berlin Olympics winning the gold medal and setting an Olympic record. Set alongside stories of the opening phases of the Spanish Civil War, the story and its headline, "Japanese Smashes Olympic Mark To Take Marathon by 600 Yards," were relatively tame.[6] Those readers with an interest in sport may have been forgiven for skipping over the comment describing the winner, Kitei Son, as a "Korean-born lad."[7]

That line is crucial, however. Japan had annexed neighboring Korea in 1910 and colonized the nation until 1945. By the time of the Berlin Olympics in 1936, Japanese rule over Korea neared the end of its third decade. For Korean Olympic hopefuls to compete in the German capital, they would have to adopt Japanese names and any victories would see a Japanese flag raised on the flagpole. Japanese authorities gave their promising marathon runner Kee Chung Son the Japanese name of "Kitei Son."

Son had been running since his childhood on the banks of the Yalu river. For him, as for many other Koreans, running was an activity that the Japanese could not directly influence.[8] Son became a medal hopeful in the years leading up to the Berlin Games and the Japanese saw in him an opportunity to demonstrate power. The marathon, after all, was one of the most prestigious disciplines at the Olympic Games. Son went to Berlin with other intentions. He wanted to show the world that Koreans could compete on the highest levels. However, after his victory, he sank into helplessness and despair as he found himself on the podium facing Japanese national symbolism. He reflected later: "For the first time, I realize the Japanese flag and the Japanese anthem (…). It is my victory. But what does this flag mean? What do the Japanese attacks on my compatriots mean? I did not run for the Japanese. I ran for myself, and for my tortured people."[9]

Son's story shows how the oppressed also can instrumentalize Olympic success for nationalist causes if sport is organized around nations. In Korea, for example, the newspaper *Dong-A Ilbo* showed Son on his frontpage days after his victory. They had erased the Japanese flag from his shirt. The incident contributed to the conflict, however. On the same day, the Japanese colonizers arrested several newspaper staff members and suspended it for several months.

It is hardly surprising then that in August 1970, the South Korean lawmaker Park Young Rok travelled to Berlin on a mission. At midnight, he approached the winner's memorial at the Olympic Stadium. Equipped with hammer and chisel, he changed the country affiliation behind Son's name from Japan to Korea. He held a short press conference the next morning to explain his actions, and left Germany again.[10] The original name was swiftly restored and the IOC made an official decision on the matter following the incident at an Executive Board meeting in 1971: a nationality of a competitor cannot be changed retrospectively.[11] The marathon victor of 1936 remains registered in Olympic statistics under his Japanese name and as a member of the Japanese team.

The stories of Kolehmainen and Son are instructive of a flag's meaning within the context of a sporting event. Kolehmainen's words tells us that the sight of the Russian flag flying and representing *him* was an insult almost worthy of losing the race. Son's case shows that flags and their meanings are ingrained as deeply within sport as they are with the nations or teams the flags purport to represent. The experiences of Son and Kolehmainen illustrate how liquid nationalities have been embedded in the fabric of the Olympic Games for much longer than we assume, challenging the static notion of national identities.

The Mhangura Meteor

Kolehmainen and Son were able to demonstrate their sporting prowess on the global stage. There is, however, a second group of athletes who became victims of the contradiction between a liquid modernity and the Olympic regulations. Those athletes' countries either did not want athletes with specific backgrounds to represent the national flag or were forced to retreat under international pressure.

In May 1970, Artwell Mandaza had run the 100 meters in 9.9 seconds. This would be no small feat today, but at the time only one athlete had officially broken the 10 seconds barrier before. He competed as one of a few black athletes for what was then known as Rhodesia – modern Zimbabwe. Obviously, Mandaza was fast, but he was prohibited from competing at the Olympic Games even though at one point he even made it to the event. What had happened?

The Mhangura Meteor, as Mandaza was known amongst his people, was born in the then British Colony of Southern Rhodesia, today's Zimbabwe, in 1946. At this point, the British had ruled over the region for 23 years. The decolonialization movements that swept through the African continent in the 1950s and 1960s also impacted British rule over the country. But rather than allowing for free elections, Rhodesia followed the "South African model" with a white minority government declaring an independent sovereign state in 1965. Segregation laws and limited political representation for black citizens were expanded and an oppressive, racial segregation system impacted all aspects of public and political life in the country until 1980.

These discriminatory laws led to sanctions from the international sporting community. Like South Africa during the Apartheid regime, Rhodesian athletes were denied access to many international sporting competitions. However, Rhodesia agreed to IOC conditions ahead of the 1972 Olympic Games, including the selection of a mixed-race team, to facilitate the nations' participation. As Robert Mugabe did in 2008 during his contested re-election, so Rhodesia sought for international recognition through the Games.

It is not a simple task to find the names of the athletes who had travelled to Munich with the Rhodesian team. Their flag, however, made it into the history books. In a video that is still available on YouTube,[12] we can see a flag-raising ceremony in the Olympic Village in Munich four days prior to the official opening ceremony. The mixed-race Rhodesian team walks into the picture, in the background a local band plays an anthem. It was customary at the time to raise a team's flag in the village on check-in. Rhodesia, including Mandaza, who had been selected based on his athletic excellence, had arrived.

The flag, however, is not recognizable as the official Rhodesian flag of 1972 that symbolized racial segregation: it was an old flag from colonial rule and the anthem played is "God Save the Queen". In order to facilitate their participation at the Games, the Rhodesians had grudgingly accepted an IOC condition to give up their national symbols. The IOC's standpoint must be interpreted as saying that colonialism was acceptable, racial segregation was not. To some, the flag did not matter. "We are ready to participate under any flag, be it the flag of the boy scouts or the Moscow flag," one team official commented. "But everyone knows very well that we are Rhodesians and will always remain Rhodesians," he continued.[13]

Flags and nationality *do* matter to the international sporting community, however. On the same day as the Rhodesian athletes marked their arrival in the Olympic village, the IOC voted to expel Rhodesia from the Games. The pressure came mainly from African NOCs, who threatened a boycott. The recorded discussions in the IOC are revealing on the matter and highlight the complexity around the focus on the nation state. Were the Rhodesians British citizens? Did they identify as British? Was the Rhodesian government illegal?[14] None of delegates appeared to have considered the consequences for the athletes. Maybe this was the reason the IOC members eventually voted to exclude the Rhodesian team from the Games after all.

Mandaza was deeply impacted by the events, arguing that he did not know what his name was or where he came from anymore.[15] The Olympics had taken away his identity, and for him the discrimination was threefold: he faced racial segregation at home, sporting exclusion away, and distancing from the black community. All he was allowed to do was to watch from the stands as Valeryi Borzov won the 100 meter final with a time of 10.14 seconds – much lower than Mandaza's personal best.

It is clear that the African NOCs were deeply concerned about systemic racism in various African countries. Four years later, many of them boycotted the 1976 Olympic Games for the same reason. However, Mandaza's destiny shows us that anti-racism campaigns had a negative, excluding impact on Black individuals. In a sporting context, the nation concept with its symbolism is at the core of this issue. It allows nations to promote a homogenized national identity and since sport organizations only collaborate with national stakeholders, they can only exclude nations as a whole. In doing so, the oppression and marginalization of individuals is only reinforced. Even by organizations' that share the same characteristics and objectives as the individuals.

Two stories stand out here. In 1980, only a few weeks after Rhodesia became Zimbabwe, the newly installed sport minister took Mandaza's various gold medals away to show them to the new Prime Minister, a man we have come across before: Robert Mugabe. Mandaza never saw his medals again, claiming that Mugabe and his ministers needed the gold.[16] The other indication of his standing came after his death in 2019. Sport administrators attended Mandaza's funeral, but the sports ministry was absent. The minister at the time was a woman we also met earlier: Kirsty Coventry, Mugabe's golden girl and the embodiment of Zimbabwe's Olympic success.[17] No surprise then that already in his lifetime Mandaza concluded: "I flew the country's flag (…) but that did not change my standing in today's society".[18]

Mandaza's case shows us that there is no divide between political office and the everyday life of citizens, including elite athletes. A 100-meter race, a football match, or a sailing event cannot be considered in isolation from governmental interests; especially not if political symbols run, play, or sail with us. Sport's adjustment to the global political structures led to the system caring more for the nation than for its athletes. Just consider, if international sport was organized around individuals rather than nations, Mandaza would most likely not have had to face double racial exclusion and it is doubtful whether Rhodesia's exclusion led to any improvements for the country's black population. He might even have won gold and become a golden boy for the country.

"We're from nowhere"

Much further north on the globe, we come across similar representation issues at the present time. Pál Joensen is one of the most successful individual athletes from the Faroe Islands. *The Independent* once portrayed him as "softly spoken, self-effacing and impossibly laid back. In short: he couldn't be more Faroese".[19] Joensen won several medals at the European Swimming Championships and competed at the World Championships under the Faroese flag. However, at the biggest sporting event of his career, the 2012 and 2016 Olympic Games, he entered the opening ceremony behind the Danish flag.

Let us consider the legal dimension first: since there is no Faroese citizenship as such, Joensen had Danish citizenship from birth. However, there is no question that Joensen does not consider himself Danish. He spoke to the press about his experiences several times. In one interview he expanded about the colors he was wearing at the Olympics and how those impacted on his performance.

> I'm used to the blue jumpsuit with the Faroese flag. So going in the full Danish kit from *Jack & Jones*, a good Danish brand, it felt kind of odd. Plus people obviously knew me in the swimming world, but did not necessarily know that I had this issue. So people were coming up to me all the time and asking: "Why are you wearing Danish clothes?" (…).

These statements, so apposite to this book's content made me curious. I decided to call Joensen and had an insightful chat with him in which he highlighted that he was a special case since he indeed identified very intensively with his Faroese roots.

> I'm pretty patriotic. So I love our national holiday. I have our national clothes for the national holidays. I teach my children the national anthem and all that, and get a little bit teary-eyed when they make their little drawings of my Faroese flag and stuff like that.

He also made statements on individualism that came close to those made by Kee Chung Son almost a century earlier.

> I also came to a realization, for to say in some respects that I'm very proud to be an Olympian, because of my achievements. I am an Olympian because of my individual achievements, and have qualified for the games individually. So, it's not the Faroes or Denmark that qualified me.

Other athletes feel the same. At the 2015 European Games in Baku, the organizers equipped Faroese swimmers with plain t-shirts and no flags at all. Their names were read out without mentioning of any nationality at all. “We were from nowhere,” participant Signhild Joensen fittingly summarized her impression.[20]

Faroese sport officials also have concerns about the use of the Danish flag. “We are geographically much closer to Scotland, Iceland and Norway than to Denmark,” one administrator told the *BBC* in 2018.[21] In some sports, they compete against all of them. Several IFs recognize the Faroe Islands. In early 2024, the men’s handball team stirred up the European Handball Championships with its performances. Four years earlier, the archipelago had 2,600 active handball players, 5% of the total population.[22] The opinion expressed by a Faroese sport official that the country wants “the same opportunity to compete in the Olympic Games under our own flag,”[23] may be part of the explanation to the controversy. Officially, the Faroe Islands competed under its handball federation at the championships, whereas at the Olympic Games it is the national flag. However, attentive viewers of the Olympic Games opening ceremony will have noticed that Puerto Rico, an unincorporated US territory with US citizens, participates under an own national flag. And so do the dependent US territories of American Samoa, Guam, and the United States Virgin Islands.

How is this possible? In the early Olympic Movement, Coubertin’s flexible and welcoming principle of “all games, all nations” allowed the certification of the NOCs from emerging nation states. The NOCs just had to oversee sport in a specific country or geographical area.[24] This was a strategic approach since the IOC strove for international recognition. South Africa or India, for example, were British colonies at the time of their recognition. However, three decades ago the IOC moved away from Coubertin’s stance on this question to protect the Games’ political neutrality. A protocol of IOC discussions in 1993 noted that any recognition of NOCs from countries such as the Faroe Islands, Macao, or Tahiti would have “incalculably serious consequences” for the IOC. This was despite the fact that those nations did “fulfill the conditions to be recognized as NOCs”.[25] On this basis, the IOC introduced a new clause in 1996, stating that an NOC can only be included in the Olympic Games after recognition as an independent country by the international community.[26] Since Puerto Rico, South Africa, or American Samoa had already been recognized by the time of the rule change, they remained in the Games. The same applied to Hong Kong, which was handed over from Britain to China in 1997. For those outside, the door had effectively been closed.

After all, what is an “independent country” and which “international community” does the IOC refer to? Since 1996, only NOCs overseeing a territory of a UN member state have been recognized. However, there is one exception. In 2014, the IOC included Kosovo's NOC, although Kosovo is not a UN Member State. Predictably, Serbia's NOC, which does not recognize Kosovo as an independent state, filed a complaint. Clearly, the lines between political and sporting matters in the Olympic Movement remain blurred. Moreover, the IOC sees itself strictly as the only institution to oversee a recognition process. In 2001, an IOC official urged IFs independently not to recognize national Faroese sport federations, for example.[27]

In 2006, at a meeting with Faroese politicians, the IOC stressed that they feared a push by twenty to twenty-five regions to become recognized if the Faroe Islands' NOC was accepted.[28] They were particularly concerned about highly-charged independent movements such as those in the Basque country or Catalonia. It appears that the Faroes' challenges are not a result of their own status but of difficulties in comparable cases. There are no problems to be expected with the Danish NOC "releasing" Faroese sport. Danish prime ministers have regularly voiced their support. For the 2024 Olympic Games, the Danish National Olympic Committee simply painted the rowing boats of Faroese Olympic athletes in blue, red, and white – without asking the IOC.

The fact that different sport organizations have opposing views makes the sport system even more diffuse. The International Paralympic Committee (IPC) *does* recognize the Faroe Islands. Faroese athletes have won a total of thirteen medals since their first participation in 1984. A cynic would recommend any aspiring Faroese athlete to make the Paralympic team to compete on the highest international level. In fact, this is a popular joke in the country.[29] Given the significant success of the Faroese national handball teams – the first sport for which the Faroe Islands became recognized by an IF in the early 1980s – the IOC might face more pressure to include the Faroe Islands in the coming Olympic cycles. It is not unlikely that the men's and women's handball teams qualify for the Olympics within the next four to eight years. What will happen then? As it stands now, the whole team could not play or would have to be represented by Denmark.

In short, like the outlined examples of athletes prior to World War One, the IOC's regulations continue to force any Faroese sporting hopeful either to compete under what is perceived to be a foreign flag or to give up their dream of competing at the Olympic Games. Similar cases can be made for athletes from, for example, Scotland, Bavaria, Catalonia, Macao, or Tahiti.

V is for Viktor

In the previous examples, IOC regulations forced athletes to compete under specific flags. I will introduce you to a different type of athlete – those who actively decided to represent a different flag than they were originally assigned.

We can return to Bauman's liquid modernity here and his argument that modern communities have lost the features of "blood" and "soil". Blood refers to family ties, whereas soil stands for the territory in which nations settled. According to Bauman, these notions were important in the origin stages of nations and nationalism. However, with the weakening of family relationships and increased national border-crossing, the two principles become increasingly outdated.[30] In a period of "liquid migration", to advance Bauman's term, the concept of national citizenship has become more temporary and flexible, and its character more unpredictable.[31]

Sport is impacted by these changes since athletes can only represent one nation in a competition. One of the recent trends that one sees in sport is the *acceptance* by athletes of a flag that is not their own and their competing under that flag in order to maximize their chances of competing at the Olympics. The trend is most prevalent in the cash-rich and oil-laden Gulf nations seeking to attract talent as a means of raising their profile in the international community.[32] Liquid modernity allows athletes to position themselves as competitive goods towards such state interests to enhance their own sporting and economic possibilities. One of them is Viktor Ahn.

Viktor Ahn was the most successful individual athlete at the 2014 Winter Olympic Games in Sochi. He won three gold and one bronze medals in short track skating. After his wins in Sochi, Ahn paraded the Russian flag during his laps of honor. The scene was markedly different from his previous Olympic successes, however. In 2006, Ahn came home from Torino with the exact same medal count, but at that time he was competing for South Korea where he was (and is) a national celebrity and superstar. Ahn is among the all-time top-6 winter Olympians and top-40 Olympic athletes in history. And he is by far the most successful athlete to feature with two national flags beside his name. This is the equivalent of Michael Phelps winning fourteen Olympic medals each for the United States and Russia.

Ahn had renounced his Korean citizenship and naturalized in Russia in 2011. Hyun Soo Ahn became Viktor Ahn. "Viktor is associated with the word victory," he said, justifying his name choice.[33] In Korea, his decision was met with anger aimed at the national skating federation. Ahn claimed that he wanted to prepare under the best possible conditions and that he had found these in Russia. He had other options. After his announcement that he would leave Korea, other Olympic powers like the US also tried to recruit him.[34]

Ahn's situation resembled a money-driven transfer market. He ended what he considered to be a contract rather than a birth tie with South Korea. Then, he solicited offers and plumped for the proposition that suited him best. In doing so, Ahn used his exceptional talent to challenge the relationship between the nation and the individual. He turned, as scholar Jin Sook Kim fittingly put it, into "the epitome of the neoliberal cosmopolitan subject".[35] As such, he also became a symbol for a growing trend in Korea. Around 14% of Korean lived abroad at the time of Ahn's move.

Ahn, however, was not an ordinary South Korean citizen, and his defection became a matter of national importance. The South Korean President, Geun Hye Park, installed a commission to investigate how the skater could have renounced his citizenship.[36] From a South Korean perspective, events in Sochi made matters even worse. The South Korean men's short track team that had collected a combined ten medals from the 2006 and 2010 Olympics, left Sochi empty-handed. Attempting to correct this sporting disaster, some news outlets cheekily added Ahn's medals to South Korea's total. Again, the question arises by whom and how a nation can be represented.

Ahn carried the trading of his talents to extremes when he coached China's short track team at the 2022 Winter Games in Beijing. He did not celebrate his team's success on the ice – the Chinese men beat South Korea for the first time in their history. The Covid-19 pandemic provided him another opportunity to show his colors, however. He simply wore a face mask painted with the Chinese flag. Ahn also quickly learned how to position himself politically. "My family and I have always supported the one-China principle. I hope to get everyone's understanding," he is said to have claimed.

Russia's military actions in the Ukraine are a measure of just how little Russian, Korean or Chinese Ahn is. At the beginning of the Ukraine war, recruitment in the Russian army became a serious prospect for Ahn. After all, he is a young man who had proved he belonged among the physically most outstanding individuals in his generation. At this moment, Ahn does not have to worry though. Ironically, his Olympic titles in 2006 freed him from the compulsory two-year military training in South Korea. He has no "military experience", which currently is a criterion in Russia's military recruitment.[37]

Ahn's case is revealing in another way, too. Many Koreans still consider him a representative of the Korean nation. A study found that Koreans reacted positive to his success in Sochi, some arguing that his blood ties run deeper than his public appearances under another flag.[38] This continuing support can be explained by people's focus on and following of individual success rather than broader political identification. Take, for example, the online fandom around football players. Cristiano Ronaldo's transfer to the Saudi Arabian club Al-Nassr got his new team over 2.5 million new Instagram followers (an increase of around 400%) within a few hours.[39] Supporters attribute an individual's success to their private commitment rather than a national sport system. Ahn represents a neoliberal individualism that is in stark contrast to global sport's set-up.

I was reminded of my own youth experiences when exploring the Ahn case. I was a teenager in the late 1990s, when Michael Schumacher began to dominate Formula 1. Watching twenty-four racing cars going round in circles together with my father on Sunday afternoon was a very important part of our weekend routines. The focus was always on "Schumi", who joined the Italian team *Ferrari* in 1996 and left the team in 2006 after 16,825 laps of racing.[40] Schumacher won 72 races for *Ferrari* and as is the custom in Formula 1, the German (for the driver) and the Italian (for the team) flags were raised after his victories to the sound of both national anthems. On many occasions, my father and I became emotional when Schumi was on the podium. That was, however, when the Italian hymn was played and the Italian flag raised. What was going on? We can learn here that humans can attach themselves to symbols other than their own if an emotional bond is created for other reasons.

It appears that we showed the same individual success patterns as the young generation of Ronaldo's Instagram followers and Korean's continuing support for Ahn. Whilst not a "nation" in an Olympic sense, the Ferrari brand represents Italy like few other brands. Ferrari allowed Schumacher to compete on the highest level, just as Russia provided Ahn with the conditions for his 2014 Olympic success. For Schumacher the realization that he represented the Italian "Ferrari nation" was a learning curve. In his early Ferrari years, he was accused of prioritizing individual over team success.[41] This changed significantly when he won five world championships in a row between 2000 and 2004. His national identities began to merge, and the emotional victory ceremonies were evidence for it. Fittingly, on the day after his last Ferrari race in 2006, the *Corriere dello Sport* headlined

"Grazie Schumi", whereas *Gazzetta dello Sport* went with "Danke Schumi". He had bridged nationalities, just as Ahn had.

The cases of Ahn and Schumacher challenge us to rethink the relationship between the nation and the individual, even though they are different in nature. Formally, Ahn was not allowed to represent both South Korea and Russia at the Olympic Games. He had to drop his Korean nationality to compete for Russia. It serves as a striking example of issues with the prioritization of the nation model in Olympic sport. In contrast, Schumacher is said to have contributed significantly to advance the relationship between Italians and Germans, precisely because Formula 1 allows transnationalism.[42] Such fluid identities – even though driven by commercialism – bears a very close resemblance to the Olympics' internationalist ambitions.

The basketballers

As a final case, we will return to the 1988 Olympic basketball final. In Chapter 3, I described the game between Yugoslavia and the Soviet Union and the team's return under the Olympic flag four years later. Now, I want to take a closer look at the individuals involved in the Soviet team to highlight how athletes can also be forced to adopt liquid national affiliations due to political events.

In the 1988 final, the top scorer for the successful Soviet Union was Šarūnas Marčiulionis. His teammate Arvydas Sabonis secured the most rebounds. Four years later in Barcelona, the two players reappeared in the bronze medal match: Marčiulionis scored the most points, Sabonis had the most rebounds. This time, however, they won their medal for Lithuania. In contrast to Russia or the Ukraine, the IOC had already granted the NOCs of the Baltic states' independent status in time for the Barcelona Games. The IOC had a historical explanation for this speedy process. The three NOCs had already received Olympic recognition in the interwar period. Marčiulionis appeared to have adopted quickly to his new colors, even attributing to them a positive effect on his performance. "It's amazing the energy that comes from playing for a new country," he later recalled.[43]

The fact that Soviet ball sport teams comprised many different regions is not new. In the 1980s, for example, the majority of footballers on Soviet football teams were from the Ukraine where the legendary Ukrainian manager, Valerij Lobanowskyj, preferred to work with Ukrainian players he knew from club football. In fact, the 1988 Soviet basketball squad included four players from Lithuania, three from the Ukraine, two from Russia, and one from each Estonia,

Latvia, and Uzbekistan. We know little about the expressions of individual player's national identities at the time, but retrospectively they made clear that they did not identify with the Soviet Union. "It was not really our country," one Lithuanian player admitted.[44]

To make matters even more interesting, the team that Marčiulionis and Sabonis helped beat for their bronze medal with Lithuania in 1992 was the "Unified Team" composed of those former Soviet republics that had not yet gained independence. Six fellow gold medalists took the floor to line up against Lithuania.

Amongst the athletes who played for the Soviet Union in 1988 and the Unified Team in 1988 was Alexander Volkov. Volkov was born in Siberia but grew up in the Ukraine. Volkov is most interesting in illustrating flexibility in national belonging in his political affiliations and his position in the current conflict between Russia and Ukraine. In the past two decades, he switched between pro-Russian and pro-Ukrainian parties several times, and he has been accused in the media of being very close to the Russian regime. However, most recently, he appeared in full military gear on social media to fight Russia's invasion of Ukraine.[45] Whether this is a sign of retaliation or of rejection of past proximity to the Putin regime is a matter of speculation, but it proves that in hostile political climates, national identities can really change direction like a flag in the wind.

It all comes together in Volkov's successful attempt to get a group of young Ukrainian basketball players out of the country to protect them from Russian attacks. The players were brought to Lithuania – where Marčiulionis and Sabonis took care of them.[46] Clearly, the identification amongst the basketball community appears to be stronger than political affiliations. Sabonis commented passionately on the Russian invasion:

> I have no idea how Ukrainians could play sports together with Russian representatives in the future. It is hard to imagine such a scenario. Now Slavs are killing Slavs. Two Slavs attacked one Slav. Cruel. Brother kills brother. It may take half a century, but the grievances will persist.[47]

The Olympics might not have actively contributed to the conflict, but the change in affiliations certainly highlights the paradox of the flag for individuals.

Conclusion

The stories I presented in this chapter span the course of over a century and come from different countries, sports, and periods. As a result, there is no uniform reaction or positioning of athletes towards flags and nationality. Some treat the flags they reject with disdain, while others were left powerless. We have also seen that some athletes defined their allegiances as loose. Clearly, differing values, histories, and personal experiences conditioned each athlete's actions. What they all have in common, however, is that they highlight the flow of individuals' national identities identified by Bauman.

In contrast, the Olympic Movement, as we have seen, continues to prioritize the nation state model as it always has. As national identities become more fluid, the rigidity of Olympic national symbolism increasingly clashes with the personal and diverse identities of athletes. Importantly though, the complexity of national representation is not new. Athletes have always been forced to be represented by national flags that they did not identify with. We know of some, like Son or Kolehmainen, but it is likely that we will never hear the stories of others.

In brief, the examples underscore the urgent need for the Olympic Movement to adapt and embrace a more flexible approach to identity. This approach must reflect the realities of a liquid modern world, where personal affiliations and identities are not bound by national borders. By embracing such a fluidity of identities, the IOC could much better represent the diverse experiences and backgrounds of athletes. This would allow us to take a step further towards an alternative way to use symbols in the Olympic Games that could involve allowing athletes to compete under more personalized or regional symbols, recognizing dual or multiple nationalities, or creating spaces for athletes to express their complex identities without being forced into a single national framework.

Notes

1 Zygmunt Bauman, *Liquid Modernity* (Cambridge: Polity Press, 2000).
2 Raffaele Poli, "The denationalization of sport: De-ethnicization of the nation and identity deterritorialization," *Sport in Society* 10, no. 4 (2007): 646–661.
3 "Q&A regarding the participation of athletes with a Russian or Belarusian passport in international competitions," *olympic.org*, October 23, 2024, https://olympics.com/ioc/media/q-a-on-solidarity-with-ukraine-sanctions-against-russia-and-belarus-and-the-status-of-athletes-from-these-countries.
4 Joost Jansen, "Nationality swapping in the Olympic Games 1978–2017: A supervised machine learning approach to analysing discourses of citizenship and nationhood," *International Review for the Sociology of Sport* 54, no. 8 (2019): 971–988.
5 Matt Llewellyn, "'The Best Distance Runner the World Has Ever Produced': Hannes Kolehmainen and the Modernisation of British Athletics," *The International Journal of the History of Sport* 29, no. 7 (2012): 1026.

6 Arthur J. Daley, "Japanese Smashes Olympic Mark To Take Marathon by 600 Yards," *New York Times*, August 10, 1936, https://www.nytimes.com/1936/08/10/archives/japanese-smashes-olympic-mark-to-take-marathon-by-600-yards-kitei.html.
7 Ibid.
8 Ron Firmite, "A hero in his native land Sohn Kee Chung is South Korea's most revered athlete. But when he won the marathon in 1936, he was a man without a country," *Sports Illustrated*, September 14, 1988, https://vault.si.com/vault/1988/09/14/a-hero-in-his-native-land-sohn-kee-chung-is-south-koreas-most-revered-athlete-but-when-he-won-the-marathon-in-1936-he-was-a-man-without-a-country.
9 Dirk Brail, "Der traurigste aller Olympiasieger," *Spiegel*, September 23, 2016, https://www.spiegel.de/geschichte/marathon-in-berlin-der-lange-lauf-von-sohn-kee-chung-olympiasieger-1936-a-1113059.html.
10 "[기고] 손기정과 박영록," *chamnews.net*, January 18, 2025, https://www.chamnews.net/news/articleView.html?idxno=65905.
11 Minutes, Meeting of the IOC Executive Board in Lausanne, March 13–14, 1971, Digital Collection "IOC Executive Board Minutes", IOC Historical Archives, Lausanne.
12 "Synd 14–8-72 Rhodesian Olympic Flag Raising at Munich Olympic Village," *YouTube*, July 23, 2015, https://www.youtube.com/watch?v=pP_agDIx7aM.
13 "1972: Rhodesia out of Olympics," *BBC*, August 22, 1972, accessed June 8, 2024, http://news.bbc.co.uk/onthisday/hi/dates/stories/august/22/newsid_3549000/3549444.stm.
14 Minutes, 1992 Session of the International Olympic Committee in Munich, August 21–24 and September 5, 1972, Digital Collection "IOC Session Minutes", IOC Historical Archives, Lausanne, 10.
15 "The man, myth, legacy," *The Sunday Mail*, October 27, 2019, https://www.sundaymail.co.zw/the-man-myth-legacy.
16 Farayi Machamire, "'I was short-changed'," *dailynews*, May 29, 2012, accessed via *Twitter* on https://twitter.com/farayimachamire/status/1186268063571812353/photo/1.
17 Tadious Manyepo, "Artwell Mandaza snubbed in death, just like in life," *The Herald*, October 24, 2019, https://www.herald.co.zw/artwell-mandaza-snubbed-in-death-just-like-in-life/.
18 Machamire, "'I was short-changed'".
19 Luke Brown, "The athletes from nowhere: Dispatches from the Faroe Islands, a proud sporting nation the Olympics won't acknowledge," *Independent*, July 26, 2018, https://www.independent.co.uk/news/long_reads/faroe-islands-olympic-recognition-ioc-the-athletes-from-nowhere-a8465436.html.
20 Ibid.
21 "Faroe Islands start campaign for Olympic recognition," *BBC*, March 8, 2018, https://www.bbc.com/sport/olympics/43327938.
22 "From goalkeeper to Prime Minister: Faroe Islands' Bárdur á Steig Nielsen," *International Handball Federation*, January 6, 2020, https://www.ihf.info/media-center/news/goalkeeper-prime-minister-faroe-islands-bardur-steig-nielsen.
23 "Faroe Islands start campaign for Olympic recognition," *BBC*.
24 Ryan Gauthier, "Statehood and the Olympic Games," *AJIL Unbound* 114 (2020): 380–384.

25 Minutes, 1993 Session of the International Olympic Committee in Monaco, September 21–24, 1993, Digital Collection "IOC Session Minutes", IOC Historical Archives, Lausanne, 100.
26 International Olympic Committee, Olympic Charter (Lausanne: International Olympic Committee, 1996), https://stillmed.olympic.org/Documents/Olympic%20Charter/Olympic_Charter_through_time/1996-Olympic_Charter.pdf.
27 Letter, Gilbert Felli to Tom Dielen December 13, 2001, File D-RM01-FEROE-002-SD1 "Demande de reconnaissance – 1989–2001", IOC Historical Archives, Lausanne.
28 *Helsingør Dagblad*, February 21, 2006, accessed via *Mediestream*, https://www2.statsbiblioteket.dk/mediestream/avis/record/doms_aviser_page%3Auuid%3A8f121f4c-c29f-4f0a-9aef-44541afa6a58/query/helsing%C3%B8r%20dagblad.
29 Brown, "The athletes from nowhere."
30 Carlo Bondoni, "Introduction to Zygmunt Bauman," *Revue Internationale de Philosophie* 277, no. 3 (2016): 281–289.
31 Godfried Engbersen, "Liquid Migration and Its Consequences for Local Integration Policies," in *Between Mobility and Migration*, eds. Peter Scholten and Mark van Ostaijen (Cham: Springer, 2018): 63–76.
32 Gijsbert Oonk, "Sport and Nationality: Towards Thick and Thin Forms of Citizenship," *National Identities* 24, no. 3 (2022): 197–215.
33 Tony Manfred, "Why A Korean Speed Skating Star Changed His Name And Started Racing For Russia," *Business Insider*, February 16, 2014, https://www.businessinsider.com/viktor-ahn-russia-2014-2.
34 Sam Borden, "Rejecting the U.S. to Skate for Russia," *New York Times*, February 9, 2014, https://www.nytimes.com/2014/02/10/sports/olympics/ahn-rejected-us-to-skate-for-russia.html.
35 Jinsook Kim, "Why We Cheer for Viktor Ahn: Changing Characteristics of Sporting Nationalism and Citizenship in South Korea in the Era of Neoliberal Globalization," *Communication & Sport* 7, no. 4 (2018) 488–509.
36 Jaeyeon Woo, "President wants to know why Olympic skater became Russian," *The Wall Street Journal*, February 14, 2014, accessed June 11, 2024, https://www.wsj.com/articles/BL-KRTB-5001
37 "18~60세 러시아男, 동원령"...빅토르안, 예외이유," *Seoul,* October 2, 2022, https://www.seoul.co.kr/news/international/2022/10/02/20221002500122.
38 Kim, "Why We Cheer for Viktor Ahn.
39 Sam Mcphail, "Own goal: Football fans' loyalty no longer lies with clubs, but players," *Spectator* 352, no. 10170 (2023).
40 "Scuderia Ferrari Hero Michael Schumacher," Ferrari, accessed June 11, 2024 https://www.ferrari.com/en-EN/formula1/michael-schumacher.
41 Christiane Oppermann, *Ferrari: das schnellste Unternehmen der Welt* (Frankfurt: Campus Verlag, 2005), 159.
42 Birgit Schönau, "Einer von ihnen," Süddeutsche Zeitung, May 10, 2010, https://www.sueddeutsche.de/sport/michael-schumacher-und-die-italiener-einer-von-ihnen-1.309017.
43 Jon Wertheim, "These Two Former NBA Players Won Gold for the USSR; Now They're Trying to Save Kids From Russian Attack," *Sports Illustrated*, April 25, 2022, https://www.si.com/nba/2022/04/25/marciulionis-volkov-players-escape-ukraine-daily-cover.

44 Bryan Kalbrosky, "The real story of why you see tie-dyed Lithuanian basketball shirts at Grateful Dead shows," *USA Today Sports*, September 5, 2022, https://ftw.usatoday.com/2022/09/the-real-story-of-why-you-see-tie-dyed-lithuanian-basketball-shirts-at-grateful-dead-shows.
45 "More Olympic medalists join Ukraine's defence: Alexander Volkov, basketball champion in Seoul 1988 with the USSR is the latest," *infobae*, March 15, 2022, https://www.infobae.com/en/2022/03/15/more-olympic-medalists-join-ukraines-defense-alexander-volkov-basketball-champion-in-seoul-1988-with-the-ussr-is-the-latest/.
46 Wertheim, "These Two Former NBA Players."
47 "Arvydas Sabonis condemns Russians: 'We'll never be able to believe these liars again'," Basketnews, March 11, 2022, https://basketnews.com/news-167825-arvydas-sabonis-condemns-russians-well-never-be-able-to-believe-these-liars-again.html.

5 Protests

> Flags reveal their true significance most profoundly when they become subjects of contention. When flags are contested, it often reflects deeper tensions and disagreements about the very essence of that collective identity and its place in society. The politics of recognition in which flags operate means that any conflicts about flags address fundamental questions of belonging, inclusion, and power within society.[1]

The scholar Catherine Baker made the above excellent observations. Baker, however, was not writing about sport when addressing the link between flags and identity. She was exploring the transnational public sphere of the Eurovision Song Contest and compared it to the music competition's nation focus. Baker's notes are important for my argumentation though. She points towards an extension of the examples I outlined in the previous section: conflicts that can be caused by flags based on diverging identities.

The IOC rules over the Olympic system. The organization can decide who – be they individuals or nations – may participate in the Olympic Games. For the Olympic system to function, however, the stakeholders involved must accept the IOC's regulations. This includes the requirements for the selection of athletes by NOCs, and the inclusion of political flags to represent them. Nations states and their powerful leaders accept, as I have shown, the symbolism around the Games as a facilitator for banal nationalism and reinforce it. Athletes appear to have no other choice than to accept the rules. Or do they?

The early chapters of Olympic history books reveal that athletes made their views heard from the very start of the Olympic Movement. Considering England's disproportionate role in colonizing nations in

DOI: 10.4324/9781003564058-5

every hemisphere, it comes as little surprise to find that one of the earliest examples of an athlete rejecting a flag at a sporting event involves the sceptered isle's oldest colony: Ireland. The athlete in question was one Peter O'Connor, who had set the world record in the long jump in 1901.[2] In 1906, O'Connor travelled with two Irish compatriots to Athens to represent Ireland at the Intercalated Olympic Games.[3] At least that is what the athletes thought. Upon the Irishmen's arrival, they were informed that a late change in the rules meant they could not compete for Ireland: the nation lacked its own NOC. They were not asked to travel back, however. Instead, they were told to represent Great Britain.[4]

The incidents that followed have been subject to various narratives and myths. O'Connor won his event and the British flag was raised for him. Fueled with Irish nationalism O'Connor himself recalled fifty years later that he clambered up the pole and replaced the flag with a green flag with the phrase "Erin Go Bragh" ("Ireland Forever"). Or so the story goes. Recent research shed light on the lack of contemporary evidence to corroborate this story.[5] Given that, according to a 2020 article in the *Irish Times,* an alleged 50,000 spectators saw the event occur, the lack of contemporary commentary is curious.[6] What is not in dispute is that Irish sport federations sent O'Connor to Athens with a flag printed with the words "Erin Go Bragh" and that O'Connor strongly disputed the idea that he represented Great Britain.

Yet it is precisely the lack of contemporary evidence set alongside the continued telling of this tale that makes the story such a striking example of the power of a flag. Over time, it ceased to matter whether O'Connor scaled a flagpole some 60 feet in the air and ripped off the British flag. The story in and of itself became a symbol of Irish antipathy towards the British, regardless of the veracity of the account. In an era long before the instantaneous sharing of photos or videos, the image conjured by the idea of the Union Jack drifting slowly towards the ground as this nimble Irishman replaced it with that of his homeland does make for a sensational and, to some in Ireland, inspirational tale of defeating the oppressor.

O'Connor was not the last. In the following, I will present other examples of athletes who showed discontent, who protested, and who broke the rules. The challenges those athletes pose to the IOC reveal further tensions with national symbolism in Olympic sports – including through flags that do not represent a nation.

The Greatest

The "Rumble in the Jungle" boxing fight between the two US American boxers George Foreman and Muhammad Ali held in Zaire in 1974 is one of the iconic moments in sport history. The fight between these two compatriots reveals opposing viewpoints towards flags of citizens of the same nation and we can learn how athletes became increasingly motivated to demonstrate their liquid relationships to their flags at sporting events.[7]

During the globally turbulent 1960s, there were few athletes who could match the global superstardom of Muhammad Ali. While his athletic feats are well known, Ali mastered the art of marketing himself, so much so that *Forbes* later called him a "World Champion in Self-Marketing and PR."[8] One of the greatest examples of Ali's ability to market himself comes from his famous fight in 1974 in Zaire that pitted him against George Foreman. The historian Lewis Erenberg wrote about the fight, "The Rumble in the Jungle represented a turning point in American culture, as the contentious forces at home and abroad came to a head in a global sporting event."[9]

A small piece of what made this fight such a cultural comment was the diametric opposition of Foreman and Ali. Foreman was an "Uncle Tom,"[10] a stereotypical, and quite-literally, flag-waving American. He had run around the Olympic boxing ring waving the American flag after his Olympic victory in 1968, days after two black Americans had been sent home for protesting about racial discrimination on the Olympic podium. Ali, in contrast, sank his gold medal from the Olympics eight years earlier in the Ohio River to protest against his nation's policies of racial segregation. In short, the two fighters represented two different but concurrent ideas at a time of extensive political protests and counter-cultural revolution within the USA. Their perspectives on the American flag were central to those opposing views.

Nothing illustrates their diverging opinions better than a dinner speech by Ali at the New York Boxing Writers' Association in the year of the Zaire fight. Ali decried Foreman as "white [and] flag-waving."[11] He continued, "[T]hose Africans are anti-America, they remember how you waved the flag at the Olympics, they don't like that."[12] Ali portrayed Foreman holding the flag as a weakness, something that should be mocked, derided. Except instead of analyzing an opponent's jab or right cross, Ali picked on what he seemed to view as Foreman's weaknesses: "white," Christian, and flag-waver.

With all eyes on the victor in Zaire, the idea was that flags would play a much greater role in the fight. Erenberg explains it as follows,

"Ali planned to wave the Zaire, Organization of African Unity [OAU], and United Nations flags in the ring to stress his worldwide popularity and make fun of Foreman's American loyalty, but [his trainer] Bundini forgot them."[13] In a match watched worldwide and broadcast to an audience of an estimated 1 billion people, Ali's plan was to mock his opponent.[14] With flags. Flags that were aimed to send a message that Ali represented certain ideas about the promotion of unity among African States. By waving the flag of the OAU, Ali sought to communicate a message of identification with certain principles, ideas and values espoused by the OAU.

Ali wanted to let the world know he was not American, he was African and proud. Ali, unlike many other athletes presented in this section, wanted to be disassociated from the values of his nation. Ali's preference was to align himself with broader, more inclusive identities and his intention to wave the flags of Zaire, the OAU, and the United Nations show his quest for a fluid identity transcending his nationality. In contrast, Foreman was an athlete as the IOC wants their athletes to be. His American patriotism represented a more static and traditional identity. Foreman aligned with established national narratives and the politics of belonging firmly rooted in American nationalism.

Ali's impact did not have any boundaries. He became arguably the first global sporting icon, and most importantly, paved the way for future Olympians to take stands on various issues including race, religion, and national belonging. As such, Ali influenced how athletes viewed their positions within society. Indirectly, he told them, you do not have to compete for a specific flag and in so doing he broadened their horizon of possibilities.

Dueling flags

Ali stood on the Olympic stage twice more. In 2012, he was brought to the London Olympic Games ceremony as a human symbol of courage and generosity. Sixteen years earlier, he took on an even more important role as he lit the Olympic torch to open the 1996 Atlanta Olympic Games. He was far away from any national symbolism, and in Atlanta, the crowd shouted his name, rather than that of his country, as he held up the Olympic torch, already visibly affected by Parkinson's disease. Four years later, at the 2000 Sydney Olympic Games, the honor to light the Olympic fire was given to Australian aboriginal athlete Cathy Freeman. Like Ali, Freeman was a high-profile athlete and an individual not aligned in her identity with the IOC's static understanding of belonging.

It is rare that individual athletes are mentioned in the IOC's official roundup of past Olympic Games. In 2001, approving the final report of the Sydney Games, this was different. Freeman is mentioned several times and praised specifically "in terms of what she had done to advance the Aboriginal cause in Australia".[15] Paradoxically, the praise for Freeman is directly linked to the demonstration of a political flag that is not an officially recognized national flag by the IOC. Freeman had sprinted her way to the gold medal in the 400-meter run a few days after the opening ceremony. As she took her victory lap, she carried with her the Aboriginal flag along with the flag of Australia. The IOC had given Australians permission to allow both flags to fly in Sydney during the Games.[16]

The permission provided Freeman with the chance to showcase her double identity, something she opted not to do at the Olympic Games in 1996. In Atlanta, Freeman had worn running shoes painted in the Aboriginal flag's colors, but not for the final run. She had also noted in her diary that she had taken the Aboriginal flag with her to the US, but she "knew that the Olympic Charter stated that no athlete could participate in anything that could be viewed as a political demonstration or he or she would risk being disqualified (…)."[17]

A comparable case where one athlete was celebrated for showcasing two national belongings occurred at the 1992 Barcelona Summer Olympic Games when the teenage boxer Oscar De La Hoya won a gold medal. Pictures immediately following the fight show De La Hoya, arms outstretched in victory, with a flag in each hand: in one the flag of the United States and in the other the Mexican flag. De La Hoya's mother had died two years prior from terminal breast cancer, an event that De La Hoya described as the "most devastating day of [his] life."[18] He wrote in his autobiography that his aunt had handed him the Mexican flag and told him as he walked to the ring, "Hold this in honor of your mother. She was Mexican."[19] According to De La Hoya, an official with the United States delegation saw the flag and told De La Hoya immediately, "If you take that [Mexican flag] up there, we are going to disqualify you. If you win, we will take the gold medal away from you."[20] De La Hoya ignored the official and waved both flags high into the air after his victory and was not punished after all.[21]

Here, we learn that the IOC appears to bypass its own regulations when it involves a particularly politically sensitive issue within the host country (as in the case of Freeman) or an emotional personal story (as in the case of De La Hoya). Especially in the case of Freeman, the IOC clearly saw more public benefit in the creation of an exception than in the potential public backlash if the Aboriginal flag had been forbidden. The privilege was swiftly reversed after the Sydney Games, however: when the aboriginal boxer Damien Hooper wore a t-shirt with a picture of the Aboriginal flag on it at the 2012 Games, he was forced to apologize for his actions.[22]

The most political flag of all

The IOC describes it as "true romance". During the 1956 Melbourne Olympic Games, at the height of the Cold War, US athlete Harold Connolly and Czech athlete Olga Fikotová fell in love. Their story, which eventually led Fikotová migrate to the California, has been discussed in research and retold in popular literature many times.[23] The story has been portrayed as one of overcoming political confrontations and Fikotová even became the US flagbearer at the 1972 Olympic Games. The IOC featured their story on a recent Valentine's Day.[24]

The love story and its political implications are not of interest to me here, however. Rather, it is the fact that the IOC markets the story on its website, in official communication, and in the Olympic Museum. The IOC seems content to instrumentalize this example of a heterosexual relationship to portray the political neutrality of the Games during the Cold War. This strategy is markedly different from the IOC's stance on the expression of other sexual or gender identities displayed in what appears to be the "most political flag of all", the pride flag.

The pride flag had its debut in 1978 at the San Francisco Gay Freedom Day Parade. The openly gay politician Harvey Milk, who was assassinated in the same year on the grounds of his sexual orientation, had urged activists to create a flag to symbolize their movement. Like a national flag, the pride flag became an element to signify a common culture and heritage. From the 1990s onwards, the pride flag then gradually emerged as a globalized symbol for the LGBTQ+ community. Today, the rainbow-colored stripes of the pride flag are the most visible queer symbol.[25]

The LGBTQ+ community is as much an imagined, constructed community of belonging as is a nation. However, it does not have a defined territory and its members do not have a shared history. Rather, the pride flag is a transnational symbol that connects the experiences of individuals beyond national borders.[26] National and ethnic belonging do not matter to the pride community, which is instead defined by sexual and gender-variant identities.[27] Those waving the pride flag claim that their form of belonging, which is not tied to the logic of a nation state, should be equally recognized. Since the community does not have a national government to defend their rights, however, they lack representation in the international arena.

The IOC classified the pride flag as a political symbol that contravenes the Olympic Charter's demand for keeping political statements outside the Olympic Games. Therefore, individuals are prohibited by the IOC's regulations from expressing sexual identities that deviate from heteronormative standards. More recently, we have seen, though, that, the IOC does not strictly enforce the rule to avoid public pressure. There are no reported punishments for athletes wearing rainbow pins or armbands at recent Games. For example, in 2014, Dutch snowboarder Cheryl Maas was not punished for wearing a rainbow glove at an Olympic event.

The IOC appears to devote more attention to the queer community. It has to. At the 2020 Tokyo Olympic Games, more than 180 out LGBTQ+ athletes participated. It is therefore reasonable to assume that an increasing number of athletes will want to display the rainbow flag at upcoming Games. The IOC will allow demonstrations of athletes' views – whether on gender or on regional allegiances – at the Olympic Games. Significantly, however, there are five "moments and locations" where this cannot happen: "the competitions on the Field of Play, the opening and closing ceremonies, the medal (or victory) ceremonies, and the Olympic Village itself".[28] Since it is in these situations that athletes receive most attention, expressions of LGBTQ+ identities remain restricted. The irony is that here only truly political, national flags are allowed.

Other organizations seem to be much further advanced. Rainbow flags were a central symbol at the opening ceremony of the 2022 Commonwealth Games. The openly gay Olympic champion Tom Daley paraded together with rainbow flags, and supporters were allowed to bring pride flags into the sport venues. To me at least, it is doubtful whether this open display of pride colors was a political gesture.

Here, too, then the IOC's framework of national symbolism only reflects a limited acceptance of identity constructs. As outlined, this framework aligns closely with traditional national identity. Significantly, in so doing the IOC also contradicts broader human rights declarations. For example, even though the United Nations has granted the IOC permanent observer status, the IOC can with its laws contravene Article 19 of the UN's Declaration of Human Rights: "Everyone has the right to freedom of opinion and expression; this right includes freedom to hold opinions without interference and to seek, receive and impart information and ideas through any media and regardless of frontiers."

We can conclude by coming back to Zygmunt Bauman's view of liquid modernity in which societal norms are constantly shifting. The rainbow flag is a strong confirmation of his theory. The Olympic Movement, however, continues to be caught on this issue between its historical roots and an interconnected community. The IOC's standpoint that the rainbow flag is too political because it does not align with the traditional system of national flags, remains rigid, not liquid.

Spectators' voices

In the past two sections, I focused on (Olympic) athletes. I do not want to omit to mention that spectators can show their discontent with flags or anthems. A quick, personal excursion into the world of football and its local identities might be useful here. In 2007, I moved to England to work and study. My choice of destination was easy – I needed to live in Liverpool. Since childhood, I had followed Liverpool Football Club and the prospect of following the team closely was tempting.

In the year prior to my move, however, I had had negative experiences with English citizens. At the 2006 FIFA World Cup in Germany, I attended a second-round game between England and Ecuador in Stuttgart. Ahead of the game, I found myself in the middle of a fight between England supporters and foreign fans that led to the arrest of 600 individuals.[29] I nearly got hit by a flying garden chair. I can still vividly recall the English group singing about the "three German bombers in the air" that were shot down by the Royal Air Force. Nationalistic tensions were running high.

I was careful when approaching football fans in Liverpool. Little did I know then that many Liverpool supporters shared my dislike of England fans. Part of the reason is the city's historical background and its large population with Irish roots. Liverpool was also one of the major ports of the British empire from which the English colonized parts of the world. In return, many immigrants moved to Liverpool and created a multicultural society from as early as the late nineteenth century. According to the author Simon Hughes, however, the major reason for Liverpool not feeling as though it is in England can be found in more recent history.[30] Hughes argues that the Conservative Party under Prime Minister Margaret Thatcher looked on in satisfaction as the city slid into decline in the 1970s and 1980s. Since this period coincides with the most successful time of Liverpool Football Club, including four European Cup wins, supporters' identification with their club and city coupled with anti-English sentiments began to define Liverpool's people.

The British Union Jack flag provides visual evidence for Hughes' argument. Liverpool supporters have a culture of taking banners and flags with them to matches. Images of the 1980s are full of Union Jack flags at Liverpool matches, particularly abroad. However, in the following decades, the flag virtually disappeared. In Liverpool online forums, individuals bringing the flag to matches are called out. The flag is considered as "dirty" and "shit".[31] Importantly, though to a lesser degree, the same is true for Liverpool's inner city rival Everton.[32]

The background of Liverpool's identification as anti-English was much in evidence in May 2023 when I took my son to his first game at Anfield. The match happened to be on the same day as British King Charles III coronation. The Premier League had demanded that all clubs play "God Save the Queen" prior to kickoff. Liverpool agreed, but their fans had other ideas. "We're not English we are Scouse" and the clubs anthem "You'll Never Walk Alone" were amongst the nicer slogans with which large parts of the stadium drowned out the British anthem. We did not hear one note of the anthem in the upper tiers of the *The Kop*. The other insults, I did not dare explaining to my 6-year-old and I will opt to leave them out here too.

Certainly, Liverpool is not the only example of such regional, rather than national ties. Catalan club FC Barcelona is another famous case. You are unlikely to encounter any Spanish national flags during matches at Barcelona's home ground Nou Camp. In the past ten years, the club's leaders have radicalized the club's position and openly promoted the Catalan region's independence from Spain.[33] When in 1992 the Olympic Games were held in Barcelona, Catalan nationalism was allowed to be on display, albeit with considerable controls.[34] However, like the Aboriginal flag, the Catalan flag is officially no longer allowed to be shown at subsequent Games.

The examples from Merseyside and Catalonia help to understand that there are also geographical alternatives to the nation concept, and local identities to be included. You might argue that the Olympic Movement differs a great deal from the world of club football. And it does. But possibly it is only the focus on a different unit that causes us largely to ignore local allegiances in the Olympics.

Let us return to China, or more precisely, to Hong Kong. Since the handover of Hong Kong from Britain to China in 1997, athletes from Hong Kong participate at the Olympic Games under the flag of the Hong Kong special administrative region. In contrast to, for example, Taiwan or the Faroe Islands, the IOC recognized Hong Kong as a self-governing system independent economically from China under the Chinese principle of "one country, two systems". It had to tie Olympic eligibility to residency, however, since Hong Kong citizens from 1997 onwards only had Chinese citizenship.[35]

Close symbolic links to China remain. In the event of a success for a Hong Kong athlete at the Olympics, the official anthem of Hong Kong is, in fact, the Chinese national anthem. This might be unsurprising considering the political significance China attributes to the Olympic arena. The Hong Kong case is therefore different from the IOC recognition of Guam and Puerto Rico, whose residents also have another nationality (US American), but where their own national flags and anthems are used at the Olympic Games.

But Hong Kong citizens are not unanimously happy with the symbolism. During the 2020 Tokyo Olympic Games, Hong Kong born fencer Cheung Ka Long won the gold medal in the men's foil competition. His final fight was streamed in shopping centers all around Hong Kong. It was the first time that an athlete from Hong Kong had won an Olympic event since the handover from Britain. When the Hong Kong flag was raised behind the podium, the Chinese anthem played. Long did not show any visible reaction, but back home, residents could not hold back their emotions. Videos of onlookers of the medal ceremony booing the national anthem in a local mall spread online like rapid fire. "We are Hong Kong" followed.[36] As in Liverpool or Catalonia, Hong Kong citizens found in the Olympics a forum to express their Hong Kong identity.

The Chinese authorities moved quickly in response to the booing and arrested individuals because of the incident. Consequences might also be felt by Hong Kong based sport associations for failing to defend the use of the Chinese anthem. In 2023, the Hong Kong Ice Hockey Association did not protest at the playing of the pro-democracy song *Glory to Hongkong* at a match in Sarajevo.[37] Here, too, political powers stepped in and threatened the suspension of the federation. That the Chinese authorities have taken such restrictive measures in recent years is no surprise. In 2020, a new national security law was introduced in response to rising unrest and pro-democracy movements in Hong Kong, a law that many critics see as a preliminary step to a total takeover of the region.

Since the 2022 Winter Olympic Games took place in Beijing, concerns have arisen that the Chinese might disallow the selection of athletes from Hong Kong who were critical of China's politics.[38] Obviously, the IOC and national sport organizations quickly offered assurances that such concerns were unfounded. It is unlikely that we will ever find out.

Conclusion

As I reflected on the connected themes of nation, identity, and symbolism discussed in this chapter, I realized that I had committed an Olympic crime. At the 2010 Winter Olympic Games in Vancouver, the first Olympics I ever attended, I had tickets for a curling session. One of the teams playing was Great Britain's women's team. All British players on the squad were from Scotland, however. Eight years earlier, gold in the event had also been won by five Scottish women – the first gold medal for Britain at the Winter Olympics since 1984. For me, an undergraduate student in England at the time, it appeared logical that I would take a Scottish flag to support them. I define my identity in sporting settings as very fluid, after all.

Little did I know that the IOC, together with the local organizing committee, forbids the display of any flag that is not from a participating country, including the Scottish flag.[39] According to the IOC's regulations, my gesture was a "political" act through which I came to politicize the sporting arena. I was lucky and my support remained unnoticed. However, aware of conflicts potentially arising at the 2012 London Olympic Games, the organizing committee adapted the rule slightly for the Games in Britain. It then read "flags of nations under the umbrella of a participating country", including "England, Scotland, and Wales".[40] In recent Games, the rule has been included in the Olympic Games' protocols without exceptions. For example, at the 2018 Winter Olympics it made it impossible for Russian citizens to bring the Russian flag since Russian athletes competed under the IOC flag. Potential punishments ranged from eviction from the stadium to police arrest. However, when the ice-hockey team of Russian Olympic athletes won the gold medal, tens of Russian flags could be seen on the stands.

The disparity between my understanding of identity and the IOC's regulatory framework is evident. The IOC's rigid policies on national symbols continue to be restrictive. My (maybe naïve) intention to bring a Scottish flag was to celebrate the personal origins of the athletes, acknowledging their specific cultural background. Paradoxically, it was the IOC's rules that interpreted my personal gesture as a political act. I only wanted to express support and appreciation for the curlers' regional origins.

Coupled with the protests outlined in this chapter, my personal anecdote therefore highlights the fact that the politicization of the Olympic arena is caused by the IOC's rules and the inclusion of national symbolism rather than by the personal and cultural expressions of identity. In doing so, the IOC continues to control the expression of national identities. It favors a simplified representation, even though my examples point to a much more complex reality. When athletes or spectators take flags, they closely identify with, their intention is not, then, to politicize sport. They are merely challenging the structures of the international sport system. Only then do flags become symbols for contestation as seen in the stories of Ali or Freeman. Only because the IOC demands that athletes compete under political flags does the Olympic arena become a platform for challenges to national identity, including a shift of attention from sport to politics.

Moving on, then, the important question remains: How can the IOC and other governing bodies of sports better accommodate the evolving identities of their participants and spectators? The IOC invented its own symbol to answer the question – the great symbol that is the Olympic flag.

Notes

1 Catherine Baker, "'If Love Was a Crime, We Would Be Criminals': The Eurovision Song Contest and the Queer International Politics of Flags," in *Eurovisions: Identity and the International Politics of the Eurovision Song Contest since 1956*, eds. Julie Kalman, Ben Wellings, and Keshia Jacotine (Singapore: Palgrave Macmillan, 2019): 175–200.
2 Frank Shouldice, "Pouring oil on the Olympic fire," *The Irish Times*, May 31, 2004, https://www.irishtimes.com/culture/pouring-oil-on-the-olympic-fire-1.1142750.
3 At the height of O'Connor's fame, that the Olympic Games would occur every four years was not a foregone conclusion. Among the issues of that era were expense, travel, and public interest. After hosting the inaugural Olympics in 1896, the Greeks sought to make Athens the permanent site, against the wishes of the Olympic Games' founder Pierre de Coubertin. While Coubertin rebuffed these initial challenges, the lengthy problems at the 1900 and 1904 Summer Olympics led the Greeks to redouble their efforts which ended in what is now known as the 1906 Intercalated Games.
4 Quote found in: Matt Llewellyn, "Lighting the Olympic Flame," *The International Journal of the History of Sport* 28, no. 5 (2011): 655.
5 Ibid. Matt Llewellyn notes the lack of contemporary sources to confirm the account, which was only relayed by O'Connor a half-century after the events occurred.
6 Ian O'Riordan, "Erin Go Bragh: A short history of Irish Olympic protest," *The Irish Times* August 1, 2020, https://www.irishtimes.com/sport/erin-go-bragh-a-short-history-of-irish-olympic-protest-1.4318739.
7 Lewis A. Erenberg, *The Rumble in the Jungle*, (Chicago: University of Chicago Press, 2019), 2–3.
8 Rainer Zeitelman, "Muhammad Ali – World Champion In Self-Marketing and PR", *Forbes,* January 20, 2020, https://www.forbes.com/sites/rainerzitelmann/2020/01/20/muhammad-aliworld-champion-in-self-marketing-and-pr/.
9 Erenberg, *The Rumble,*2–3.

10 "Ali Beating Drums for TV Tickets," *New York Times,* August 30, 1974, https://www.nytimes.com/1974/08/30/archives/ali-beating-drums-for-tv-tickets.html.
11 Dave Anderson, "Broken Glasses at the Waldorf," *New York Times* June 24, 1974, https://www.nytimes.com/1974/06/24/archives/broken-glasses-at-the-waldorf-dave-anderson-more-laughs-at-first.html.
12 Ibid.
13 Lewis A. Erenberg, "'Rumble in the Jungle': Muhammad Ali vs. George Foreman in the Age of Global Spectacle" *Journal of Sport History* 39, no. 1 (2012): 81–97.
14 "Mike Tyson May Fight George Foreman In Biggest Money Match: $80 Million For Winner," *Jet,* September 18, 1995, https://books.google.com/books?id=fTkDAAAAMBAJ&pg=PA46#v=onepage&q&f=false.
15 Minutes, 2001 Session of the International Olympic Committee in Moscow, July 13–16, 2001, Digital Collection "IOC Session Minutes", IOC Historical Archives, Lausanne, 45.
16 John Pye, "Freeman's legacy endures long after Sydney's flame went out," *Associated Press,* August 14, 2020, https://apnews.com/article/australia-race-and-ethnicity-sports-asia-2020-tokyo-olympics-sydney-e618ee6002e8a48e3d45581562268f80.
17 Gary Osmond and Matthew Klugman, "A Forgotten Picture: Race, Photographs and Cathy Freeman at the Northcote Koori Mural," *Journal of Australian Studies* 43, no. 2 (2019): 203–217.
18 Oscar De La Hoya with Steve Springer, *American Son: My Story* (Harper Collins: New York, 2008), 5.
19 Ibid., 19.
20 Ibid.
21 "Gold medalist De La Hoya Becomes a Media Star," *Los Angeles Times,* September 10, 1992, https://www.latimes.com/archives/la-xpm-1992-09-10-ti-10-story.html.
22 "Rule 50 Guidelines," *Olympic.org*, accessed April 3, 2021, https://stillmedab.olympic.org/media/Document%20Library/OlympicOrg/News/2020/01/Rule-50-Guidelines-Tokyo-2020.pdf.
23 Mark Dyreson, "The Californization of Olympian Love: Olga Fikotová and Harold Connolly's Cold War Romance," *Journal of Sport History* 46, no. 1 (2019): 36–61.
24 "East-West romance in Melbourne," *Olympic.org*, February 13, 2021, https://olympics.com/en/news/blast-from-the-past-east-west-romance-in-melbourne.
25 Sarah E. Chinn, "Queer Feelings/Feeling Queer: A Conversation with Heather Love About Politics, Teaching, and the 'Dark, Tender Thrills of Affect'," *Transformations* 22, no. 2 (2012): 124–131.
26 Pia Laskar, Anna Johansson and Diana Mulinari, "Decolonising the Rainbow Flag," *Culture Unbound. Journal of Current Cultural Research* 8, no. 3 (2016): 192–217.
27 Baker, "'If Love Was a Crime, We Would Be Criminals'."
28 "IOC EB approves one change of nationality and Guidelines on Athlete Expression for Paris 2024," *olympic.org*, January 18, 2024, https://olympics.com/ioc/news/ioc-eb-approves-one-change-of-nationality-and-guidelines-on-athlete-expression-for-paris-2024.

29 "Schwere Ausschreitungen in Stuttgart," *Frankfurter Allgemeine Zeitung*, June 15, 2006, https://www.faz.net/aktuell/sport/fussball-wm-2006/deutschland-und-die-wm/sicherheit-schwere-ausschreitungen-in-stuttgart-1332418.html.
30 Simon Hughes, *There She Goes: Liverpool, A City on its Own. The Long Decade: 1979–1993* (Liverpool: deCoubertin Books, 2019).
31 @Murf, "Re: Flags on Wednesday," Redandwhitekop Forum, April 14, 2005, 11:45 a.m., https://www.redandwhitekop.com/forum/index.php?topic=55933.320.
32 Tony Evans, *Two Tribes. Liverpool, Everton and a City on the Brink* (London: Bantam Press, 2018).
33 César García, "Nationalism, Identity, and Fan Relationship Building in Barcelona Football Club," *International Journal of Sport Communication* 5, no. 1 (2012): 1–15.
34 John Hargreaves, *Freedom for Catalonia? Catalan Nationalism, Spanish Identity and the Barcelona Olympic Games* (New York: Cambridge University Press, 2000).
35 Minutes, 1997 Session of the International Olympic Committee in Lausanne, September 3–6, 1997, Digital Collection "IOC Session Minutes", IOC Historical Archives, Lausanne, 88f.
36 "Hong Kong man arrested for allegedly booing Chinese anthem while watching Olympics," *The Guardian*, July 21, 2021, https://www.theguardian.com/world/2021/jul/31/hong-kong-man-arrested-for-allegedly-booing-chinese-anthem-while-watching-olympics.
37 Geoff Berkeley, "Hong Kong NOC issues 'written reprimand' to ice hockey body over anthem blunder," *insidethegames*, May 20, 2023, https://www.insidethegames.biz/articles/1137159/hong-kong-ice-hockey-body-reprimand.
38 Naaman Zhou, "'We are Hong Kong': can the Olympics sidestep the politicisation of sport in China?," *The Guardian*, October 26, 2021, https://www.theguardian.com/world/2021/oct/26/we-are-hong-kong-can-the-olympics-sidestep-the-politicisation-of-sport-in-china.
39 City of Vancouver, Olympics Protocol Manual (Vancouver: City of Vancouver, 2012).
40 Quoted in: Baker, "'If Love Was a Crime, We Would Be Criminals'."

6 The Great Symbol's Shortcomings

We have now established that the use of national flags in international sport, but particularly in the Olympic Games, can be considered a contradiction on many levels. However, national flags are not the only symbols in international politics or sport. Sport organizations like FIFA have their own flags. The Premier League uses flags with its commercial logo. With such symbolism, these bodies also promote a brand or visualize an identity as national flags do.[1]

Due to the value that we attach to such international flags, their use becomes problematic when they become associated with specific groups that are not allowed to use their national flags. Take the example of international chess, which is run by the World Chess Federation (FIDE). The Russian invasion in Ukraine led the federation to ban the Russian national flag from its competitions. Grand masters like the Russian-born Ian Nepomniachtchi were instead invited to play under the "neutral" flag of the federation. But does this association between Nepomniachtchi, who is considered by Putin as an important national asset to regain the world chess title for the country, not indicate that he is closer to the federation and the FIDE flag than all the other players? Possibly, this was an intended move. At the time of writing, the federation's president is the Russian Arkady Dvorkovich, a former assistant to Putin.[2] At the very least, the case raises the question of whether the flags of sport organizations can be considered neutral at all.

The IOC also has its own "great symbol", the Olympic flag. Using that flag for athletes without a clear national affiliation has been an option for the IOC in the past. NOCs have also opted for this solution at various points to disassociate their athletes from political issues. We already learned earlier that at the 1980 Moscow Olympic Games, for example, several NOCs used the Olympic flag at the opening and at medal ceremonies. This led to an unusual sight following the

DOI: 10.4324/9781003564058-6

individual pursuit in men's cycling. The riders from Switzerland, France, and Denmark were all represented by the Olympic flag that then appeared three times above their heads.[3] This incident points to another major issue with the Olympic flag: if flags are meant to demarcate, then what is the point of using a neutral flag in the first place?

The following pages delve into some well-known, and some not so well-known, controversies around the Olympic flag. As I will show, at two points in the past 60 years the questions regarding national flags became so time-consuming and polarizing that the IOC briefly considered doing away with national flags altogether and just having teams use the Olympic flag, as briefly described in the introduction of the book.

The Olympic Flag

The Olympic flag, as it is commonly known, represents like no other Olympic symbol the sport movement's internationalist objective. Given the political tensions ahead of the First World War, Pierre de Coubertin saw himself forced to invent an own symbol for the Olympic Movement. The IOC first discussed a model of a flag in 1910 and again in 1913.[4] Until today no one knows what this model looked like. However, Coubertin and his fellow IOC members rejected the proposal and instead the French Baron took the matter into his own hands. He experimented with various designs in the IOC's first headquarters, based in the home of his parents in Paris. In summer 1913 he was satisfied and presented his own design of a new logo and described his ideas in the *Olympic Review*. The logo now had its five interlaced rings, representing the five parts of the world with the six colors, including the white background, reproducing the colors of all the nations' flags.

I regard his decision already as an admission that political symbolism was misleading the Olympic idea. The inclusion of the colors of all the nations' flags points towards such an assumption, too. Coubertin wrote about the colors:

> the six colors combined in this way reproduce the colors of every country without exception. The blue and yellow of Sweden, the blue and white of Greece, the tricolor flags of France, England, the United States, Germany, Belgium, Italy and Hungary, and the yellow and red of Spain are included, as are the innovative flags of Brazil and Australia, and those of ancient Japan and modern China.[5]

Coubertin's argumentation for the five colors is insightful. He only includes the flags of those nations that had participated at the Olympic Games until 1912. Certainly, Coubertin could not have foreseen the designs of future national flags, but contrary to general belief, the rings do not represent the colors of all present nations anymore. For example, citizens of the Republic of Ireland and India will struggle to find the iconic orange color of their national flags. The color purple is also absent from the Olympic flag. The Olympic flag actually symbolizes the status of nation state recognition more than one hundred years ago at a time when the Games were not yet claiming to be neutral.

As with so many other important issues, Coubertin did not wait for approval from his IOC members but decided to use the new logo immediately. In July and August 1913, he began using the new logo on his letterhead. Something else is striking about Coubertin's introduction of the Olympic flag in the *Olympic Review*. He positions it clearly as a peace symbol against the realities of a looming war. Coubertin thereby argues that his newly-created flag "eloquently evokes both conquered terrain and guaranteed endurance".[6] In other words, the rings symbolize the universal and timeless mission of the Olympic Movement, and according to the current *Olympic Charter* "all individuals and entities who are inspired by the values of Olympism" can participate in the Olympic Games.[7] However, this statement is not correct. Only a small number of elite athletes who qualified are able to compete at the Games.

Due to the cancellation of the Games in 1916, it would take another seven years before the Olympic flag was first hoisted at an Olympic event at the 1920 Antwerp Olympic Games. Then, it was stolen, or at least, that is what the IOC and a regretful robber made the public believe. In the late 1990s, the then oldest living Olympic medal winner Hal Haig Prieste claimed that he had climbed the flagpole, stole the flag and kept it in a suitcase for more than seven centuries.[8] Others, such as Australian swimmer Dawn Fraser, later imitated Prieste's actions. Fraser was arrested on the last night of the 1964 Tokyo Olympic Games for pulling an Olympic flag from the Emperor's Palace.[9] She was released because, ironically, she was the flagbearer of the Australian national flag during the Closing Ceremony on the next day.

In prevalent attempts to enlist sport for nationalist purposes, the Olympic flag became quickly instrumentalized, too. The United States Olympic Committee, for example, produced a large number of Olympic flags around the time of the First World War. According to

Coubertin, the flags were given to "universities and associations in the New World as a symbol of the perennial nature of Olympism, and of the upcoming resumption of these solemn celebrations". But it also shows that the flag was used as a political device as the United States aspired to expand its political interests around the globe.

Against this background, the positioning of the Olympic flag as a neutral political symbol is problematic. Flags always symbolize something and can be utilized by different stakeholders to attach their own meanings to them. We should also not forget that the Olympic flags with the rings has become the brand logo of the Olympic world. The Olympics became a commodity, bought by sponsors and television, and the Olympic flag became the exclusive symbol for ownership of the Olympic product.

"A flag that waves for their rights"

The Olympic flag has become a lifeboat for the IOC since the Second World War. The organization itself now instrumentalizes the rings as a representative symbol for selected individuals who have no national flag of their own. In recent years, the Olympic flag has become most visible as part of the Refugee Olympic Team.

The idea of including a refugee team goes back to 1952 when the China question and political pressure threatened the staging of the Olympic Games for the first time. The IOC rejected the application pointing to its own rules that would not allow it.[10] Athletes were required to represent a nation. In 1976, several athletes African NOCs that boycotted the Montreal Olympic Games sought support from the IOC to participate as individual athletes. Their request was rejected, too.

IOC president Thomas Bach broke with tradition when he announced the formation of the Refugee Olympic Team for the 2016 Olympic Games. The initiative marked the first attempt to unify stateless athletes under one flag.[11] The team comprised athletes who had resettled in new countries but were not yet citizens. The refugee team opened up an avenue for them to compete at the Olympics. Despite the obvious ethical dilemma present in denying refugees the right to compete, the concept of refugees competing at the Olympics does seem at odds with the history of the Olympics' self-promotion and global branding. As journalist Uri Friedman phrased it, "[I]n a competition that typically celebrates national successes, the Refugee Olympic Team highlights national failure."[12] The refugee athletes competed under the Olympic flag. The flag choice was taken by an organization, the IOC, that wanted to be seen as humanitarian amidst the global refugee crisis. In other words, against the background of the Olympic rings' commodification, the Refugee Team was a marketing stunt.

Alternatives existed. The refugee Yara Said had created an orange flag with a thin black stripe across the middle that represents the "Refugee Nation".[13] She found inspiration in her traumatizing journey from Syria to Europe: "Black and orange is a symbol of solidarity with all these brave souls that had to wear life-vests to cross the sea to look for safety in a new country," she stated,[14] While attempts to have the flag sanctioned to represent the refugee team failed, the Refugee Nation still sent flags down to Rio with the aim that some supporters would raise awareness by waving the flag.[15]

The introduction of the refugee team was also a strategic move to circumvent challenges regarding individual athletes. At the 2012 London Olympic Games, the IOC had to deal with the case of the marathon runner Guor Marial. He had fled South Sudan during the Sudanese civil war and ended up in the United States. When he ran the Olympic qualifying time in 2011, the IOC and the Sudanese government leaned on him to represent Sudan. Marial, who had eight siblings killed by Sudanese government forces, refused. After an international campaign to pressure the IOC to allow Murial to run under the Olympic flag, the IOC relented. "To run under the Olympic flag," Murial said, "I feel like I'm representing the whole world."[16] Such an interpretation of the symbolism of the Olympic flag is understandable. However, Murial did not represent the entire world. He represented those athletes who did not fit into the IOC's dominant understanding of a world composed of nation states.

Four years later, the IOC apparently asked South Sudan permission to include five athletes who had formerly represented the country in what was now the Refugee Olympic Team for the 2016 Olympic Games. This was accepted and led to the curious case of five South Sudanese nationals competing as refugees while the South Sudan NOC also participated with three athletes at the Games. The IOC asked and received approval from South Sudan for the athletes to join the Refugee Olympic Team. It shows that the IOC carefully navigates the introduction of the new team in an effort to uphold the discourse of the nation state. The same applies to IOC funding for the initiative. It is provided to NOCs to identify and support athletes.[17] National sovereignty – national politics – continues to play a crucial role, even while the rhetoric around the refugees points to the exact opposite.

The paradox, however, is obvious. South Sudan's NOC, like any other former home NOC of refugee athletes, is no longer formally responsible because of their refugee status. How would the IOC have reacted, had South Sudan rejected the request? The IOC could not have forced the NOC to act without the risk of withdrawal and therewith violating its own principles and product. Had the IOC included the athletes anyway, it would have reduced its initial approach to absurdity. In addition, the IOC in its approach to the issue in some cases collaborates with regimes that caused the conditions for refugees to flee in the first place.

Athletes, too, have refused to acknowledge to be represented by the Olympic flag. In October 2015, the IOC banned Kuwait's NOC. At issue was a law in Kuwait that allowed for government interference in sport organizations, which contradicts the IOC's rules. What is notable about the ban is how the IOC handled the Kuwaiti athletes who would compete at the Rio Games. Rather than banning Kuwait's athletes from competing at the Olympic Games altogether, the IOC made the concession to allow Kuwaiti athletes to compete under the Olympic flag, just like the refugees. One athlete, a Kuwaiti army officer named Faheed Al-Deehani, competed in Rio in a shooting competition trap and won gold. Following his victory, Al-Deehani dedicated his victory to Kuwait saying, "That was for my country, for the people who don't want us to participate in the Olympics."[18] Further, Al-Deehani rejected the idea of carrying the Olympic flag during the Opening Ceremonies. He told the media in his home nation, "I am a military man and I will only carry the Kuwaiti flag."[19] Al-Deehani was not the only athlete from Kuwait in Rio. 52-year-old Abdullah Al-Rashidi competed in the skeet shooting competition, winning the bronze medal. As he did not have a national team uniform, Al-Rashidi competed in a jersey from the English Premier League team Arsenal Football Club. When asked later if he wore the jersey because he supported Arsenal, Al-Rashidi answered simply, "I don't know. I just bought it."[20] Al-Rashidi was more forthcoming in his opinion at not seeing the flag of his home nation flying during his medal ceremony. He said, "Anybody who doesn't see his flag, he dies. I need my flag, this is better for me. But what can I do?"[21]

Al-Deehani and Al-Rashidi's refusal to be associated with the Olympic flag underscores the simple fact that individuals attach different meanings to flags. The refugee athlete Guor Marial thought he presented the entire world when he competed under the five Olympic rings. For the Kuwaiti athletes, the exact same flag symbolized betrayal of their country. In addition, how can they reject Olympic symbolism and still continue to participate at the Olympic Games that promotes the values the athletes seem to distance themselves from? Clearly, the contradictions of flag use in the Olympic Movement also include the Olympic flag.

Four missing votes

During a 1957 meeting between the IOC and NOCs, Dutch representatives made a courageous proposal that could have been proposed in the book you are reading. The Dutch suggested that the parade of nations should be removed from the opening ceremony and replaced by the athletes marching under sport groups. National symbols should also be removed and replaced with the Olympic anthem and flag at victory ceremonies.[22] Instant opposition came from a nation that was in the midst of politicizing the Olympic Games as a demonstration of political power, the United States. "A march by sports groups would not thrill the spectators in the same manner as the present march by nations, it would be drab and lack enthusiasm," reads the recorded objection. He went on to comment on the anthem issue: "I think that everybody was thrilled when Barthel of Luxembourg won the 1,500 meters in Helsinki and the anthem of his small country, never heard before, was played in the stadium."[23] Apparently, spectator preferences were the main reasons why national symbolism had to be maintained. I hear this argument a lot when I discuss with sport enthusiasts the possibility of national flag removal. "Who should I support?" and "Why would I watch?" are common questions.

However, several years and political incidents in international sport later, the 1960s proved to be the decade in which we came closest to a removal of national flags from international sport. Sport administrators appeared tired of the debates around recognition of the two Chinas, Germanys, and Koreas. Sport's politicization by the Cold War superpowers further raised concerns about the relationship between sport and politics. In some cases, sport organizations experimented at events. In 1969, a European diving competition did not feature any flags and anthems either, leading to boycotts by several Eastern bloc states, including the Soviet Union and East Germany.[24] Earlier that year, they reacted the same way at the wrestling championships. To those countries, the flags were now more important than the athletes, even though the IOC, precisely in response to such politicization, had introduced the discourse of division between sport and national politics.

The 1963 World Skating Championships left the most lasting impression.[25] Here, too, national flags and anthems were not used. Tsuneyoshi Takeda, then President of the Japanese Skating Federation and later an IOC member, proposed the same principle for the 1964 Tokyo Olympic Games. He thought that the removal of flags would lead to a "truly friendly atmosphere stressing individual competition".[26] Unsurprisingly, he found support from a Taiwanese colleague who considered the constant flying of the US and Soviet flags at sport events a "too strong color of nationalism".[27] National representatives coming together within the framework of *World Athletics* also discussed and experimented without flags. The European Youth Athletics Championships in 1968 did not include flags. Athletes instead competed for their national federations.[28] Athletics and skating did not continue their brave initiatives beyond those individual cases.

Why did they revert? We find some answers if we look more closely at recorded discussions within the IOC. The Olympic historian Volker Kluge has published a very detailed article on the discussion of a potential removal of national flags and anthems during victories at the end of the 1960s.[29] I do not want to repeat his findings in full here but it is worth revisiting some of the arguments that were exchanged at the time.

As outlined in this book's introduction, the German president of the International Olympic Academy, Prince Georg of Hanover, advanced the first serious written proposal for flag removal in 1968. He provided three main reasons: (1) hoisting national flags are contrary to the aim to overcome national differences; (2) the national flag at victory ceremony distracts the public's attention away from the personality of the victorious athlete; and (3) there was an inflation of flag parades and national anthems due to the increasing number of competitions.[30] In light of some of the challenges I discussed in this book, you must be nodding in approval of his concerns.

The subsequent discussions amongst IOC members could have provided fascinating insights into the dynamics within the IOC and would have helped us understand why the proposal was eventually rejected. However, the IOC minutes do not detail them.[31] Nigeria's Adegboyega Ademola's support for the reform is the only personal opinion noted. We also learn that Jan Staubo of Norway and Reginald Alexander of Kenya spoke in favor. IOC President Brundage was more pragmatic than he had been fifteen years earlier and reported that the NOCs were generally against the suggestion. This information, however, is important. The NOCs obviously represent their nations and therefore it appears understandable that they wanted to keep the national symbolism. In fact, it was exactly for this reason that Coubertin had structured the IOC around individuals and not national representatives.

It appears that some IOC members understood their role, because there was in fact a majority for the Prince of Hanover's proposal: 34

voted for the abolition of flags and anthems, and only 22 against. However, because the proposal would have required a change in the Olympic Charter, four votes were missing to achieve a two-thirds majority. The Prince still had hopes that he would eventually see the end of national symbols at the Olympic Games as he noted: "The times of national pathos are nearing their end".[32]

As we have learned earlier, he was wrong. The next four summer Olympics Games were the most politicized ever: terrorism, boycotts, and political power plays remained the main topics on the IOC's agenda. Against the background of the boycott threats around the 1980 Olympic Games, the IOC discussed the removal of national flags for a second time and more seriously. There were several leading proponents of eliminating national flags and utilizing the Olympic flag for all delegations. One was Finnish IOC member Paavo Honkajurri. He despaired of the encroaching political considerations within the Olympic Movement and wrote to his IOC colleagues: "Athletes are now being forced more and more into representing their own countries than taking part in the Games for the sake of sport itself."[33] Honkajurri had identified national flags and anthems promoting this increase in nationalism present at the Olympic Games. He also suggested to replace them with Olympic symbols such as the Olympic flag and the Olympic anthem. Honkajurri even offered a prediction as to what would happen if the IOC were to follow this course of action: removing national flags for the Olympic flag, would "disengage politics from Olympic sport at a single stroke."[34]

As in the late 1960s, there was support for the suggestion. French IOC member Malik M'Baye, for example, asked his colleagues to do away with national flags and anthems by changing the Olympic Charter. In his written proposal, he argued that politics had begun to "menace" the Olympic Movement and that one way to limit the influence of politics would be to remove national anthems and flags during the medal ceremonies. "[D]o away with these displays of chauvinism," he urged.[35] M'Baye was not alone in this stance. Daniel Plattner of Switzerland made a similar point that possibly best encapsulates the problem around flags: "Such a change [the removal of national flags] would have nothing at all to do with the honor of a country (…) victory ceremonies are meant for victors and not for nations."[36]

American IOC member Julian Roosevelt had an idea that avoided eliminating the use of national flags at the Olympic Games but rather limiting their use. He outlined his ideas to IOC president Juan Antonio Samaranch in August 1980, days after the Closing Ceremonies for the Moscow Summer Olympics. Roosevelt believed in flying national flags from the Olympic Village in order to identify which teams were participating but eliminating national flags from the competition venues. As for medal ceremonies, Roosevelt argued for retaining the national flags but eliminating the use of national anthems. He believed this course of action would "reduce the nationalistic display" while "retain[ing] some national identification for the teams attending."[37]

In short, the IOC had already seriously considered the removal of all national flags twice in over its history. In both instances, many IOC members spoke in favor. In 1968, the proposal even gained a convincing, though not large enough, majority. The discussions came in times of crisis, but the national flags remain a central feature in the Olympic Games until today. The flags were protected during the discussions by those IOC members who interpreted their roles most fervently as national representatives. The entire Eastern bloc spoke out against removal, for example. Their representatives wrapped up their arguments in the notion that the raising of flags during the medal ceremony served to educate the youth of the world.[38]

In the following years, the debates ebbed away as the IOC turned towards commerce and the national flags became a crucial part of the Olympic DNA to be sold to sponsors and television broadcasters alike. They became part of the Olympic brand, whilst the rhetoric of neutrality was advanced in parallel, culminating in the adoption of "political neutrality" among the fundamental principles of Olympism in the Olympic Charter in 2019.

The Youth Olympic about-turn

Over history, the IOC has made other, smaller admissions that the national symbolism might indeed have no place at the Olympic Games. Two initiatives stand out, but these also faced opposition and demonstrate that national symbols remained of primary importance to the majority of decision-makers within the IOC.

The first is the closing ceremony of the Olympic Games, at which you have surely noticed that athletes do not march in as part of their national delegations. They mingle together. The national flags of all participating NOCs still make an appearance, however, as they are paraded into the stadium separately.

The IOC introduced the mixed set-up for the first time in 1956. The idea came from a then thirteen-year-old Chinese schoolboy, who had written a letter to the IOC. He had hoped that the alternative format would contribute to the depoliticization of the Olympic Games. Aware of potential resistance, the IOC President Avery Brundage kept the suggestion secret and worked with the Australian organizing committee behind the scenes. In many public outlets, the surprising new feature received positive feedback. In the IOC, however, not everyone was pleased. In subsequent IOC Executive Board meetings, members voiced concerned about the lack of order and thought the mixed march was "a very unpleasing aspect".[39] Others complained that Brundage had moved without informing the Board.[40] Clearly, the more often athletes were associated with national symbols, the better, many thought.

A second example is the Youth Olympic Games (YOG). This event at which young elite athletes between the age of fourteen and eighteen participate was introduced in 2007. The first YOG took place in Singapore in 2010.[41] The introduction of the YOG was a reaction to a declining interest of young people in the Olympic Movement. The then IOC President Jacques Rogge was the main driving force behind its establishment.[42]

For example, the YOG included innovative competition formats such as three-on-three basketball that were thought to be more appealing to young people. Significantly, it also challenged the national representation criteria through a few mixed-NOC team events. In this format, athletes are randomly drawn into teams with athletes from other countries, for example in mixed-relay events. The organizers use the Olympic flag for all teams in the mixed-NOC events.

Originally, IOC President Rogge wanted to go even further. In an interview with *L'Equipe* a few months before the IOC vote on the introduction of the YOG, he had explained that the event was to make a decisive step away from national representation: "Only one thing will be different," he explained. "There will be no national flags and anthems to avoid all nationalism. The only flag raised during the medal ceremonies will be the Olympic flag, and the only anthem will be the Olympic anthem."[43] Rogge was prepared to enforce this change at the YOG, the project he considered to be his presidential legacy.

We do not know what it was that changed Rogge's mind within only a few weeks. During the 2007 IOC Session, he made a complete about-turn:

> They had to be innovative. They had to get children away from computers get them playing sport. The national flags were a must. In his experience, the young athletes had great pride in competing for their country, and loved seeing their national flag hoisted.[44]

Despite the need for innovation, Rogge now thought that national symbolism should remain untouched. Maybe his change of faith was caused by other IOC members highlighting the importance of young elite athletes' learning to represent a nation from an early age. The IOC member Francesco Ricci Bitti, for example, compared the YOG to a youth tennis event in their attempts to "increase awareness of the value of representing one's country".[45]

It was a missed chance. Instead, politics began to matter from the very first YOG edition in 2010. When 17-year-old Gili Heimovitz entered the arena for his final in the 48kg taekwondo competition, notably behind a sign with the Israeli flag, his opponent Mohammad Soleimani was missing.[46] Heimovitz then steps onto the mat, bows to the referee, and is handed an Israeli flag that he waves to a group of around fifty spectators. When Heimovitz returns around ten minutes later for the medal ceremony at which the Israeli flag is raised and the country's anthem played, Soleimani remains absent. IOC officials and the Iranian delegation say Soleimani was injured.

It is hard to believe that Soleimani was indeed unable to be at the competition site due to injury. Iran has a state policy that prevents Iranian athletes competing against Israeli opponents in the international arena. It claims that such a sporting contest under the respective two flags would recognize Israel as a sovereign state, which the Iran fiercely rejects. Soleimani, then 16 years old, became a victim of his state's political stance. Heimovitz, too, found himself facing questions and narrowed the issue down to the national flags: "to stand on the podium and listen to the Israeli anthem and see the Israeli flag over the Iranian flag" appeared to be intolerable from an Iranian perspective.[47]

In light of the incident, the YOG were indeed a missed opportunity. Rogge's about-turn triggered precisely what he had intended to do away with through a removal of political symbolism: nationalist sentiments.

Conclusion

In this chapter, I attempted to show the undeniable influence of nationalism at the Olympic Games by shifting perspective and focusing on Olympic symbolism. We have seen that the Olympic flag highlights a gap between the ideal and the real. Like a national flag, the Olympic flag is not just a passive symbol but actively stands for the political dynamics of the times. The rejection of the athletes who did not want to be represented by the Olympic flag shows once again that flags are multifaceted. Clearly, there remains a gap between the idealistic aims of the Olympic Movement and the realpolitik of international sport. Just imagine the not unlikely scenario for future Olympics where Russia is still at war with Ukraine, China attacks Taiwan, an epic refugee wave rolls over Europe, and several Arab nations invade Israel. Would all these nations and individuals be allowed to compete under the Olympic flag of peace and unity? I doubt it.

We can return to East Asia for a final time for an illustration of how even specially created flags can cause conflicts. At the 2000, 2004, and 2018 Olympic Games, the delegations of North and South Korea marched into the opening ceremonies together. In all three instances, the IOC had played an active role in the negotiations between the two countries that are technically still at war.[48] The staged peace demonstration served the IOC well in its desperate attempt to demonstrate symbols of unity at the Olympic Games. Since an official "unification flag" exist on the Korean peninsula, it became quickly evident that this flag – displaying the geographical borders of the Korean peninsula – would be used.[49] It is far less widely known that the joint Korean appearance had been financed by the South Korean IOC member Un Young Kim, who paid his North Korean counterpart Ung Chang, and therewith indirectly the North Korean regime, around one million dollars.[50]

In 2000, the flag elicited no conflict, but in 2003, the disputed Liancourt Rocks were added to demonstrate Korean ownership of the territory. The Liancourt Rocks, known as *Dokdo* in Korean and *Takeshima* in Japanese, have been a bone of contention between South Korea and Japan for more than a hundred years. The Japanese government protested against the inclusion of the dots on the Korean flag for the opening ceremonies in 2004 and 2018. Japan succeeded. The IOC recommended the removal of the islands from the flag because the situation around the island's status was "political". Controversially, the IOC did not apply the same pressure ahead of the 2020(1) Tokyo Olympic Games when the islands appeared on the maps of the Olympic torch relay and in other official Olympic material.[51] We see the IOC's selective application of the politicization argument continued.

Notes

1 Catherine Baker, "'If Love Was a Crime, We Would Be Criminals': The Eurovision Song Contest and the Queer International Politics of Flags," in *Eurovisions: Identity and the International Politics of the Eurovision Song*

Contest since 1956, eds. Julie Kalman, Ben Wellings, and Keshia Jacotine (Singapore: Palgrave Macmillan, 2019): 175–200.

2 Jörg Krieger, Andrew Hao and Tabea Gering, "International Sport Federations as Forums to Initiate Soft Power Processes: The Case of Russia," *Asian Journal of Sport History and Culture* 2, no. 1 (2023): 1–24.

3 Philip Barker, "As they celebrate their centenary, how the Olympic rings have become the most famous symbol in the world," *insidethegames*, June 22, 2014, https://www.insidethegames.biz/articles/1020882/as-they-celebrate-their-centenary-how-the-olympic-rings-have-become-the-most-famous-symbol-in-the-world.

4 Karl Lennartz, "The Story of the Rings," *Journal of Olympic History* 10 (2002): 29–61.

5 Pierre de Coubertin, "The Emblem and the Flag of 1914", in *Olympism. Selected Writings*, ed. Norbert Müller (Lausanne: International Olympic Committee, 2000), 594.

6 Ibid.

7 International Olympic Committee, Olympic Charter (Lausanne: International Olympic Committee, 2023), https://stillmed.olympics.com/media/Document%20Library/OlympicOrg/General/EN-Olympic-Charter.pdf.

8 Historians have shown how Prieste's flag could not have been the piece of cloth on the flagpole, however: it had a different size. It seems that the IOC – always looking for a good story – fell for Prieste's acting talent. Before and after his Olympic career, he had featured in various films and stage shows, possibly learning from fictional thieves. In fact, there are no records of a successful stealing of the first Olympic flag, but a failed one where robbers were caught by the police. See: Lennartz, "The Story of the Rings."

9 Dawn Fraser with Harry Gordon, *Below the surface. The confessions of an Olympic champion* (Galway: MW Books, 1965).

10 Toby C. Rider, "The CIA, the IOC, and the Efforts to Establish a Refugee Olympic Team," *Journal of Olympic History* 24, no. 2 (2016): 36–42.

11 Rebecca Davis, "Refugee Olympic Team: How Symbols of a Crisis Got to the Games," *NBC News,* August 2, 2016, https://www.nbcnews.com/storyline/team-refugees/peace-run-rio-story-refugee-olympic-team-n617241.

12 Uri Friedmann, "Rio 2016: Where Refugees Are Finally Being Recognized," *The Atlantic*, August 10, 2016, https://www.theatlantic.com/international/archive/2016/08/refugee-olympic-team-rio/494969/.

13 The Refugee Nation, "The Refugee Nation – Official Video," *YouTube*, July 20, 2016, https://www.youtube.com/watch?v=Dkby9BmYrXQ. There was a separate attempt in 2015 by a California real-estate agent to crowdfund a new nation for refugees that went by the same name. According to Amnesty International, their efforts are "not affiliated at all with an effort … to advocate for a new nation to be created for refugees." Quote found in "Amnesty International Rallies Behind Refugee Athletes Competing in Olympic Games," *Amnesty USA*, August 4, 2016, https://www.amnestyusa.org/press-releases/amnesty-international-rallies-behind-refugee-athletes-competing-in-olympic-games/.

14 "Our Flag," *The Refugee Nation*, accessed April 29, 2021, http://www.therefugeenation.com/#OurFlag.

15 Natasha Saunders and Faye Donnelly, "The Refugee Olympic Team at Rio 2016: rallying around which flag?" *Open Democracy*, March 10, 2017,

https://www.opendemocracy.net/en/refugee-olympic-team-at-rio-2016-rallying-around-which-flag/.

16 Laura Padoan, "Guor Marial: the refugee marathon man running for the world," *UNCHR,* August 14, 2012, https://www.unhcr.org/en-us/news/latest/2012/8/502a51979/guor-marial-refugee-marathon-man-running-world.html.

17 "Olympic Solidarity 2021–2024 Plan Refugee Athlete Support Program Guidelines," *canoeicf.com*, accessed June 10, 2024, https://www.canoeicf.com/sites/default/files/refugee_athlete_support.pdf.

18 John Marshall, "Kuwait's Al-Deehani wins double trap gold as independent," *AP*, August 11, 2016, https://apnews.com/article/ce12a953d8ac4e07b2b0e3133f5f3b24.

19 Agence France-Presse, "Fehaid al-Deehani: Man who refused to carry IOC flag, wins gold for Kuwait," *Hindustan Times,* August 11, 2016, https://www.hindustantimes.com/olympics/fehaid-al-deehani-man-who-refused-to-carry-ioc-flag-wins-gold-for-kuwait/story-M3E4h6fazYpwdHDT9RB6hJ.html.

20 Mary Milliken, "Shooting: Mustache! Brazilian fans adopt man with no country," *Reuters,* August 14, 2016, https://www.reuters.com/article/us-olympics-rio-shooting-mustache/shooting-mustache-brazilian-fans-adopt-man-with-no-country-idUSKCN10O0WS.

21 Ibid.

22 Minutes, Meeting of the Executive Board of the IOC with Delegates from National Olympic Committees, June 7–8, 1957, Digital Collection "IOC Meetings with NOCs", IOC Historical Archives, Lausanne, 12.

23 Ibid.

24 "East Bloc Boycotts Bolzano," *Herald Tribune*, August 20, 1969, Folder "Flags & Hymns – Question of Discontinuing Use in Victory Ceremonies 1956, 1963–1969," Film 56, Avery Brundage Digital Collection, University of Illinois Archives.

25 "No Flags or Anthems at Olympics Suggested," *The Asian Student*, March 16, 1963, Folder "Flags & Hymns – Question of Discontinuing Use in Victory Ceremonies 1956, 1963–1969," Film 56, Avery Brundage Digital Collection, University of Illinois Archives.

26 Ibid.

27 Ibid.

28 Minutes, Meeting of the IAAF Council in Frankfurt, February 24–25, 1968, Collection "IAAF Council Meeting Protocols", World Athletics Archives, Monaco, 17–18.

29 Volker Kluge, "A Piece of Cloth and a Melody – a Never Ending Struggle," *Journal of Olympic History* 28, no, 3 (2018): 25–35.

30 Minutes, 1968 Session of the International Olympic Committee in Mexico City, October 7–11, 1968, IOC Session Minutes, IOC Historical Archives, Lausanne, 57

31 Ibid., 14.

32 Kluge, "A Piece of Cloth and a Melody".

33 Minutes, 1980 Session of the International Olympic Committee in Lake Placid, February 11–13, 1980, IOC Session Minutes, IOC Historical Archives, Lausanne, 45.

34 Ibid.

35 Minutes, 1980 Session of the International Olympic Committee in Moscow, July 15 – August 3, 1980, IOC Session Minutes, IOC Historical Archives, Lausanne, 36.
36 International Olympic Committee, *11th Olympic Congress in Baden-Baden* (Lausanne: International Olympic Committee, 1981), 70.
37 Letter found in: Minutes, Meeting of the IOC Executive Board in Lausanne, October 30–31, 1980, Digital Collection "IOC Executive Board Minutes", IOC Historical Archives, Lausanne.
38 Minutes, 1980 Session of the International Olympic Committee in Moscow, 36.
39 Minutes, Meeting of the IOC Executive Board in Evian, June 3, 1957, Digital Collection "IOC Executive Board Minutes", IOC Historical Archives, Lausanne, 5.
40 Minutes, Meeting of the IOC Executive Board in Paris, October 2, 1959, Digital Collection "IOC Executive Board Minutes", IOC Historical Archives, Lausanne.
41 Jörg Krieger, "Fastest, highest, youngest? Analysing the athlete's experience of the Singapore Youth Olympic Games," *International Review for the Sociology of Sport* 48, no. 6 (2012): 706–719.
42 Svein Erik Nordhagen and Jon Helge Lesjø, "Rogge's Games: Establishing the Youth Olympic Games as a New Event in the Olympic Movement," *The International Journal of the History of Sport* 35, no. 11 (2018): 1091–1110.
43 "Rogge Offers More Details on Youth Olympic Games," *Around The Rings*, July 8, 2021, https://www.infobae.com/aroundtherings/ioc/2021/07/09/rogge-offers-more-details-on-youth-olympic-games/.
44 Minutes, 2007 Session of the International Olympic Committee in Guatemala City, July 4–7, 2007, IOC Session Minutes, IOC Historical Archives, Lausanne, 57.
45 Ibid., 54.
46 "Women's -44kg and Men's 48kg Finals – Taekwondo | 2010 YOG Singapore," *Olympics.com*, accessed June 12, 2024, https://olympics.com/en/video/women-s-44kg-and-men-s-48kg-finals-taekwondo-2010-yog-singapore.
47 "Politics Pollute Inaugural Youth Olympic Games," *Athletic Business*, August 16, 2010, https://www.athleticbusiness.com/operations/legal/article/15143033/politics-pollute-inaugural-youth-olympic-games.
48 Jung Woo Lee, "Olympic Ceremony and Diplomacy: South Korean, North Korean, and British Media Coverage of the 2018 Olympic Winter Games' Opening and Closing Ceremonies," *Communication & Sport* 9, no. 5 (2021): 761–784. Also see: Ki Woon Kim and Hee Jin Seo, "Tracing Two South Korean Olympic Pathways: Symbols, Conflicts, and Integration through Global Sports Events" *The International Journal of the History of Sport* 39, no. 11 (2022): 1284–1302.
49 "Japan protests unified Korea Olympic flag with disputed isles," *AFP News*, February 5, 2018, https://sg.news.yahoo.com/japan-protests-unified-korea-olympic-flag-disputed-isles-053025909.html.
50 Ibid.
51 Joseph Egidio, "Japan and South Korea's battle over Dokdo/Takeshima at the Olympics," *EastAsiaForum*, October 9, 2021, https://eastasiaforum.org/2021/10/09/japan-and-south-koreas-battle-over-dokdo-takeshima-at-the-olympics/.

7 Proposing New Olympic Visions

A Thought Experiment

We have now arrived at the point where, I believe, we can confidently conclude that the use flags, whether as national or as international symbols, within the Olympic arena poses significant challenges to the alleged political neutrality of sport. How could this issue be overcome?

I already addressed my bold conclusions to this question in the first chapter to spark your curiosity and reflection. I noted, first, that national flags should be removed from the sporting arenas during competition. Second, athletes should be entered in the Olympic Games as individuals, detached as much as possible from their nationalities or citizenships.

There is, of course, another obvious alternative: a reversal of the claim that emerged from Cold War times that the Olympic Games must be politically neutral. Current IOC President Thomas Bach continually repeats the adage that sport should be neutral, often referring to Coubertin. However, Coubertin spoke about peace, a principle that in our current times of violent conflict appears to be more important to embrace than neutrality. Such an admission would allow stakeholders of sport to rightfully remove militant, aggressive nation states from the Olympic Movement. For example, a complete ban of Russia from competing at the Olympic Games based on the horrendous human rights violations the Putin regime has committed during the war in Ukraine would easily be justifiable. While potentially coming at the cost of universal participation, such a stance would mean a more truthful adherence to sport's values as they were intended by Coubertin.

However, rather than a move in this direction, the IOC has tightened its stance on political neutrality over the past decades. These actions culminated in the codification of political neutrality as a "Fundamental Principle" of the *Olympic Charter* in 2019. Hence, other alternatives should be elaborated.

DOI: 10.4324/9781003564058-7

A sign of things to come?

Maybe sport organizations have already taken note of the expanding paradox? A new urge amongst sport organizations emerged in the past few years: name changes. For example, the International Association of Athletics Federations was transformed into World Athletics, the International Swimming Federation became World Aquatics, the International Badminton Federation changed its name to Badminton World Federation, and the International Rowing Federation is now known as World Rowing. The reasons for these modifications are multiple and include improved marketing possibilities, disassociation with past scandals, and mergers of previously separate institutions. Amusingly, World Taekwondo Federation's switch to World Taekwondo was forced by the former acronym's association with a vulgar phrase: W(hat) T(he) F(—).[1]

What all these relabeling processes have in common is the abandonment of the term "international". World Athletics argued that the organization's nature was easier to understand without the inclusion of the term, particularly when engaging with a younger audience.[2] Others have reasoned that the term "world" is more inclusive and avoids reference to the relations and interactions between nations as sport continues to deny a link to politics.

Moreover, newly emerging frameworks for organizing international sport also avoid a structure around nations. Between 2017 and 2019, the International Swimming League (ISL) challenged the global swimming monopoly of World Aquatics with the introduction of a privately funded professional team-based competition. The Ukrainian-Russian billionaire Konstantin Grigorishin finances ISL. Based on the North American sports model with drafting and private teams, the first ISL season went ahead in 2019 following a dispute between the two organizations. Interestingly, discussion centered around whether the ISL was "international".[3] World Aquatics argued that despite the absence of national affiliations, the ISL event was classified as international because it contained mainly "foreign" participants. For international events, World Aquatics had a six-month approval window that had elapsed before the ISL's announcement of the new league. World Athletics threatened to ban all athletes who wanted to compete at the ISL event for two years.

It is bad enough that World Aquatics moved against athletes, the weakest link in the global sport system.[4] Many prominent athletes were brave, however, and called out World Aquatics: ban of us if you dare, we will be competing at the ISL events.[5] What is even more relevant here is that the nation principle was used to justify the monopoly over the sport of swimming. World Aquatics is set up as an organization comprised of 209 member federations.[6] We also find national flags displayed on the website.

Imagining and specifying alternatives

The above developments could be read as a sign of things to come and appear to be a first step towards a different organization of global sport. Similarly, more than a decade ago the sport historians John Gleaves and Matt Llewellyn had already suggested that in sport "national allegiance should no longer play a primary role" and "international sport is a cultural artifact whose time has passed".[7] They argue that we should speak about *inter-national* rather than *international* sport. The former is characterized by athletes representing their countries, whereas the latter by definition involves people from more than one nation, but they do not necessarily compete against each other based on national affiliation.

However, taking into consideration the historical challenges outlined in this book, can we imagine a more radical alternative? It is here that I ask you to consider broadening your horizon of possibilities for the future of international sport and experiment with the thought of a complete removal of national symbols.

1 The Olympic locker

We might have to admit from the outset that the forces who would want to keep the national flags and the parade of nations as part of the opening ceremonies are probably too strong. After all, national governments invest – often heavily – in elite sport. However, the political symbols could be presented independently and separated from the introduction of the athletes, like the present custom at the closing ceremonies. Many NOCs would favor such a solution. The athletes who participate at the opening ceremonies often have to wait for many hours before they can enter the stadium with their national delegations. Such waiting times might have a negative impact on their preparation for their competitions. In Tokyo, for example, the Danish delegation walked in with only 26 athletes and officials, even though it had more than 120 athletes at the Games. Australian athletes voiced similar concerns ahead of the 2024 Olympic Games.[8] Instead, the ceremony can be left to the host country and the politicians – if needed.

Alternatively, the flags can be brought into the stadium by volunteers, or other individuals who have contributed to local (sporting) communities. This would demonstrate the Olympic Movement's focus on humanitarianism as intended by its founders and reflect the recently updated Olympic motto "Faster, Higher, Stronger – Together".

Then, the flags should literally be locked away. Once the flags have entered the stadium and – if needed – have been greeted by head of states on the stands, a gigantic locker could be presented in the middle of the Olympic stadium. The flags could be put into the locker by the voluntary flagbearers. Once all flags are in, the IOC President locks the flags, and therewith symbolically all national sentiments, away for the duration of the Games. At the closing ceremony, they can reappear and then parade out into their political arenas again.

Since the flags would disappear for the duration of the Games, it would also matter much less which flag is "recognized" by the IOC. A flag would not have to be attached to an NOC. Regional flags could equally enter the Olympic locker. After all, it is those groups who would be happy to lock their national sentiments *away* that can participate. We create the opposite effect from the current situation where groups with their symbols strive to be seen on the Olympic platforms. In other words, if you accept that your flag is locked away during the sport competitions, it can be included in the opening ceremony.

2 *Victories for individuals*

During the medal ceremonies, the focus should then also solely be on the Olympic athletes and their individual achievements. I believe it is not too far-fetched to envision that instead of hoisting national flags and playing nation anthems, athletes (and onlookers) look up to a video of their career's achievements, potentially with family, friends, coaches, or others who supported their careers. Prior to their competitions, they could select a song to be played with it. This could be a compilation for teams consisting of several players, too. We know that during medal ceremonies, athletes experience deep emotions. But are we, and athletes, tricked to believe that the emotions are only caused by the national symbols? In my view, athletes and our identifications with them can equally be caused by them showing emotions towards those close to them.

Who do Oscar or other movie award-winners thank? I have rarely heard them acknowledging their nations. Flags are not raised, anthems remain silent in Hollywood, no matter how patriotic a movie production might have been. Instead, in their speeches the winners express their feelings to other actors, the directors, support staff, and often their close family and friends. Karima Benzema in his earlier referenced Balon d'Or speech also spoke about his family and so did Pál Joensen in my interview. We have also learned about Michael Schumacher's relationship to the Italian flag. But Italians only started to fall for him when, in 2003, his mother had passed away a day before a race. Schumacher won the race and cried uncontrollably on the podium. "The hero had become a human," the *Süddeutsche Zeitung* interpreted the scene later.[9] When it came to his family, his mother, he showed the strongest emotions.

The IOC might have moved into this direction already. At the 2020 Tokyo Olympic Games spectators, as well as family members, were banned from attending the Olympic events due to the Covid-19 pandemic. The IOC set up opportunities right next to the competitions for athletes to speak to their families after their performances. This led to emotional scenes with athletes bursting out in tears when they heard words of encouragement or praise from their families. In addition, at recent Olympic Games medals have often been awarded to the athletes at separate events in the host's city center. At the 2024 Paris Olympic Games, the organizers set up a Champions Park in front of the Eiffel Tower that allows the athletes to celebrate together with fans, family, and friends after their competitions. The feature also aims to bring the athletes closer to the local population and is less intended for television viewing. Emotions are generated here more through the connection between athlete and spectators, and much less through the national symbols, as is often argued.

Critics might throw in that athletes from restrictive regimes such as Russia could not freely chose the contents of their videos. However, if we detach the athletes from national representation, such political interference could diminish. Moreover, even if there is some manipulation, it would be less political than the current use of the national flag.

3 *Offering alternative visions to athletes*

This book's focus on the fate of individual athletes and decisions around national flags has shown that there were plenty of incidents in Olympic history where the system in place was too static and inflexible. What I have not mentioned, yet, is that there were also athletes who wanted to give up national flags altogether.

In 1980, for example, British swimmer Duncan Goodhew voiced his concern about national flags amidst threats of boycott and NOCs picking their own logos over national flags. Goodhew reasoned: "I feel it is necessary for the sake of sport to become devoid of politics and I personally am prepared to forfeit the Union Jack and national anthem for the sake of sports and I think and I hope that other athletes will agree with me on that point."[10] When in 1976 African nations left the Montreal Games to boycott the participation of New Zealand, individual athletes pleaded with the IOC to participate as individuals. Guyana's sprinter James Gilkes later remembered that he was denied this opportunity by the IOC – a decision that Gilkes considered a political act in itself.[11]

Many will argue that athletes have a strong desire to represent their nations and compete under their national flags. This is probably true. But have they been provided with serious alternatives? Maybe they are simply accustomed to representing a nation and have never considered any other formats? We can only be certain that they would not be equally (or more) eager to represent a continent, a fantasy team, or a region, if they had experienced such situations at the Olympic Games.

Maybe they would prefer to compete for the unit of a civilization as proposed by Samuel Huntington?[12] He argued that the primary source of conflict in the post-Cold War world would not be ideological or economic, but cultural. He believed that global politics would be dominated by interactions between major civilizations: Western, Confucian, Japanese, Islamic, Hindu, Slavic-Orthodox, Latin American, and possibly African civilizations. For example, this could be an alternative for Muslim women on the French Olympic team at the 2024 Olympic Games. France has a strict secularism in place for individuals in public duty, which forbids the wearing of a hijab at the Games.[13] This regulation forces Muslim women to decide between nation and religion. Yet, if they were not to be considered official representatives of the French nation symbolized through the French flag, they could make an individual decision.

By engaging with alternative visions we broaden the horizon of possibilities for athletes to consider other representation formats. We cannot rightly argue that flags should stay because athletes celebrate their nations if they have not properly been afforded alternatives. They need to be provided with triggers to develop their imaginative capabilities, an open-endedness, to engage with.

Importantly, none of the alternative formats would prevent the athletes' experiencing the Olympic Games as the social movement fostering intercultural collaboration that Pierre de Coubertin intended. He thought that elite athletes should experience sport and culture at the highest levels and then serve as role models in this system as they pass on their experiences at the Games to their local communities. Such cultural exchange mainly takes place in the Olympic Village. Here, the

athletes can engage with each other outside the global spotlight: speak, eat, and play with each other. Flags are hoisted in the Olympic villages on arrival of national delegations, too. But the athletes stay here as individuals. If national flags and national affiliations were to disappear from the Olympic Games, it would only have a minimal effect on life in the village. The scholar Bruce Kidd has argued, for example, that every Olympic athlete should be required to live in the Village and be encouraged to participate in intercultural activities.[14]

Such a requirement is in place for the young athletes at the YOG. In my earlier work, I interviewed and analyzed athletes' experiences at the YOG and it became very obvious that most enjoyed life in the village.[15] It was here that they engaged with youngsters from all over the world. The athletes interviewed preferred the spontaneous exchanges in the village to the cultural and education programs that the organizers had created for them.

The exchanges in the Olympic villages might even be very intimate. In March 2024, French media reported that the Olympic organizers will hand out 220,000 free condoms to athletes in the Olympic Village. This tradition started at the 1988 Seoul Olympic Games to raise awareness about HIV/AIDS. At the Olympics in Rio, the number peaked at 350,000 condoms – more than thirty condoms for each athlete.[16] I doubt that the condoms are marked with national flags. A removal of flags from the Games, will do the "cultural" exchanges no harm.

4 Addressing economic and popularity concerns

For most of us, entertaining the ideas outlined here might still lack an adequate address of a potential negative impact on the economy and popularity of the Olympic Games. Let me therefore turn to this likely objection. In fact, when I presented the proposal of flag removal at a recent meeting of the European Council in May 2024, politicians immediately voiced such concerns. This was predictable, of course. But, if nation states are only in the game for the political symbolism, are they not revealing that they were deceiving the international sport community in the first place? Moreover, historically sport policy and investments have largely focused on sports and elite performances despite the need for more focus on leisure sports and physical activity.[17] This might be a possibility to initiate such a policy change.

Moreover, there is no reason to believe that the elite athletes would suddenly stop being role models for healthy living and promoters of physical activities amongst a broader public, which is the most common justification for governments to invest in elite sport. Positive health outcomes could still be promoted through continued financing, and so could national sports programs that teach life skills or resilience.

In addition, in contrast to the Olympic Movement's foundation period, the great majority of national sport organizations such as NOCs or national sport federations have their own corporate logos today. They might include national colors and symbols, but they are not the representation of the political entity that is the nation state per se. They could still be used, for example on the athletes' outfits.

The removal of flags and nations does not have to stop the IOC's support of national sport movements either. Between 2021 and 2024, the IOC paid $590 million to national sport programs via its Olympic Solidarity program. In addition, each NOC receives a direct share of income from the IOC's revenues. Such payments could still take place and possibly transfer funds directly to governments based on a transparent publication of the funds' use.

Another alternative could be the implementation of direct shares of Olympic revenue to participating athletes. Such a proposal was proposed by the German independent athlete representation group Athleten Deutschland in 2019. Athletes all over the world apparently support this demand, with 57% of the respondents in a representative survey agreeing that the IOC should pay the athletes directly.[18]

The esports phenomenon illustrates that there are large communities who follow competitions without the involvement of nations and flags. A removal of the flag and nation constructs with their associated simplification could trigger viewers to make more informed choices about which athlete to cheer for, as is the case in sport. Currently, most people consider their allegiances as a given through the framework that international sport provides. In the new concept, viewers could no longer simply rely on the nation construct that had been put in front of him for decades. Sympathies for an athlete could still be based on nationality. But could equally be based on their style of play, which really would put sporting performances at the center. Criteria other than nationality could be prioritized if, for example, athletes had to pick a song to be played at the victory ceremony, rather than the national anthem, and had to declare it before competition, spectators could cheer for an athlete based on her song collection. Maybe the Danish tennis player Caroline Wozniacki would pick Neil Diamond's "Sweet Caroline". Surely, many Olympic spectators outside Denmark would love to hear the song, and most likely it would also trigger intense emotions in Wozniacki. Rather than supporting Wozniacki via a constructed nationhood, individuals could make their own choice and simultaneously loosen themselves from political symbolism.

Television could also include children and youth more actively in creative attempts to demarcate athletes from each other. They could stage digital drawing competitions with created symbols that athletes and teams could pick from. One could envision such an initiative as a tribute to Pierre de Coubertin once again. He had considered the element of beauty/art as a core principle of his philosophical Olympism.[19] Most prominently in football, but also in other sports, federations and organizers already use children as player escorts. Those children are heavily branded with logos of major sponsors such as *Lidl* or *McDonalds.* [20] The children serve, therefore, more as alienated commercial advertising boards then as a commitment to youth engagement. In contrast, the IOC could involve them, together with the media, as contributing actively to the construction of new, individual symbols at the Olympic Games.

In fact, there might even be an economic advantage for the IOC. As regards potential commercial exploitation of the Games, the IOC clings firmly to the principle of keeping commercial advertisements out of Olympic sporting venues. Here, the IOC argues, the sole focus should be on athletes' performances, to facilitate an inclusive and equality promoting atmosphere. You will not even see advertisements of the IOC's main sponsors such as *Coca-Cola, Panasonic*, or *Alibaba* in the Olympic sporting venues. This makes the use of national symbols even more paradoxical, since it means that, for example, communist symbols are preferred over any association with an Olympic sponsor. If national flags were also to disappear, the focus on the athletes could increase even further. In addition, the Olympic flags would become the only flag allowed in the Olympic arenas, raising its exclusivity and value. It could be a good reason for the IOC to increase financial contributions in negotiations with television broadcasters and sponsors that want to pay for the use of the rings. In fact, since no "political" symbols would be allowed inside the venues, the IOC could also make a much more justifiable claim to keep rainbow flags or other statements of identity out of the Games. Athletes would have to accept that they cannot themselves bring flags to competition venues. The victory lap would have to be done without a national flag – but with full focus on the athletes' emotions instead.

5 The team sport complexity

I understand that the matter is a little more complex for team sports. In this final step of the thought experiment, we are therefore challenged to consider even more far-fetched scenarios.

In some sports such as football, basketball, and rugby, the Olympic Games are not the main international event. In football, the most skilled players are absent from Olympic competitions. This is rooted in history, as FIFA created its own World Cup in the 1930s as the organization disagreed with the Olympic amateur rules. Today, FIFA continues to protect the exclusivity of the World Cup. It rules that the Olympic football tournament is be contested by under-23 players, including three older players who can join each team.

Often, international federations that oversee ball sports also recognize more national federations than the IOC does NOCs. For example, Northern Ireland, Scotland, and Wales have separate national teams that are capable of qualification for major international or continental events. For the 2012 Olympics, however, players from those federations had to be integrated into the Great Britain football team.[21] I have also already mentioned the possibility that the Faroe Islands' handball teams might qualify for an Olympic tournament in the future. They have no opportunity to join under the current framework, however.

I invite you to imagine a total break-up of competition formats. Players can also be selected on an individual basis. In the NBA, for example, there is an all-stars weekend which receives significant attention. Players compete as individuals in skills challenges such as three-point competitions. They then play a match between players organized in Eastern and Western US states. The responsible IFs might support such a format since it would significantly increase the standing of their own world championships, held in the traditional competition format. Moreover, it would solve issues such as the participation of Faroese athletes, who could continue to compete in ball sports under the IF framework with individual athletes participating in skill challenges or similar.

It seems that such innovations are indeed slowly emerging in football. In summer 2024, the broadcaster *DAZN* started a new *Infinity League* with the aim of reforming football. The games are played on an interactive glass floor that has been used in NBA all-star weekends. The teams consist of male and female players, legendary retired footballers, youth players, and content creators as the event aims to blend different worlds of football.[22] In fact, the IOC piloted an individual event in ball sports at the Youth Olympic Games. The ice-hockey skills challenge, for example, tested players in disciplines like fastest lap, shooting accuracy, passing precision, and puck control.[23] Importantly, qualification for the event was on an individual basis.

If we want to stick with the "real" team sport product, it would still be possible to mix the teams and not let national teams play at the

Olympic Games. The international federation could draw all registered individual players – nominated by fellow players, the public, coaches – into random teams a few weeks ahead of the Games. Surely, this would also lead to attention that television could exploit financially. It could even increase youth appeal. In the virtual football game FC24, formerly run as FIFA, a strong focus is on trading player cards to compile the best possible team. It is not unlikely that young gamers could identify more with a liquid format in Olympic sports than the rigid nation state structure. Players would also be challenged to adapt to new teammates within a short period of time. Competitions could include fantasy names like "It's getting Messi", "Murder on Zidane's floor", or "Chicken Mo Salah", which are already amongst the funniest and most popular fantasy football team names.

Conclusion

Taken together, the removal of national flags from the Olympic Games could democratize the Olympic Movement and make the Games more about the athletes and less about nations. This change would align with the original Olympic spirit envisioned by Coubertin, which emphasized peace and intercultural exchange over national rivalry. In my view, such a proposal fosters a sense of global community and shared humanity, rather than reinforcing divisions. Throughout the book, I showed how the persistent use of national flags at the Olympics undermines the event's supposed political neutrality and its pacifist aims, navigates the complexities of a liquid modernity, and perpetuates outdated nationalistic sentiments. The maxim of the Olympic vision must be peaceful, athletic competition, and removing national flags could significantly contribute to this goal.

In Coubertin's day and age, the need to classify nations was useful to find backing for his Olympic idea. Moreover, peaceful international exchange between people was reduced to events such as world fairs and the Olympic Games, and the "other" was still far distanced. This has changed today when – through technological and media developments – we can be in contact with other cultures with a couple of finger clicks. Moreover, the Olympic Games have attained the universalism Coubertin envisioned. Therefore, the national symbols of flags (and anthems) are no longer required to demarcate nations. Instead, they signify the dangers of nationalism.

Certainly, the proposition to remove national flags from the Olympic Games from the ceremonies and challenging the nation state concept, disturbs deeply rooted Olympic traditions and raises significant implications for the future of international sport. To me, however, such a radical reform would best facilitate the promotion of an inclusive, individualized, and politically neutral celebration of athletic excellence. The proposed practical solutions for ceremonies, such as using volunteers to carry flags and symbolically locking away national symbols during the Games also focuses on humanitarian values.

The initial step involves detaching national flags from the opening and closing ceremonies. This change would shift the focus from nations to the athletes themselves. Instead of parading under national banners, athletes could be introduced individually or in groups based on other affiliations, such as their sport or even their personal stories. This alteration aims to preserve the ceremonial grandeur while reducing the emphasis on nationalistic displays.

The second step is the complete removal of national flags from the Olympic Games, including during competitions and medal ceremonies. This would mark a profound shift towards a focus on individual excellence and the pure spirit of competition. Athletes' achievements would be celebrated through personalized symbols or selected songs, emphasizing their personal journeys and the support systems that have contributed to their success. Such a move acknowledges the increasingly fluid and adaptable nature of contemporary life, best summarized in Bauman's concept of "liquid modernity." By moving away from rigid national affiliations and adopting such a transformative approach, the Olympic Games can reflect this modern fluidity, celebrating athletes as individuals in a global, interconnected context rather than as representatives of fixed national entities. And at the same time, such a transformative approach would also honor the original ideals of the Olympic Movement.

Historical developments and ongoing issues in global sport have taught us that sport leaders, athletes, spectators, and other individuals in elite sport have created deep relationships towards national flags. Our imaginative capabilities, to use Yuval Noah Harari's framework, allowed us to develop such links. However, we have also seen that the symbolism of flags is nothing less than a myth and that our perceptions of who and what an individual flag represents can differ significantly.

What we have done here is to challenge a relationship that is so deeply entrenched in our thinking about the Olympics. But there is no reason *not* to challenge this, and this was the exercise undertaken in this book. Therefore, I have a final question for you, one that was also my first, and one that I would encourage you to debate in other forums: Can you imagine the Olympic Games without national flags?

Notes

1 "WTF Rebrands to World Taekwondo," *World Taekwondo*, June 23, 2017, http://www.worldtaekwondo.org/wtnews/view.html?nid=29223&mcd=C03&page=13.
2 Duncan Mackay, "IAAF officially agree to change name to World Athletics after debate," September 26, 2019, https://www.insidethegames.biz/articles/1085180/iaaf-to-change-name-to-world-athletics#:~:text=Adille%20Sumariwalla%2C%20the%20Indian%20who,the%20youth%2C%22%20he%20said.
3 Jared Anderson, "FINA Rule Introduction Could Outlaw Energy for Swim Meet," *Swimswam*, November 2, 2018, https://swimswam.com/fina-rule-interpretation-could-outlaw-energy-for-swim-meet/.
4 Helen Lenskyj, *The Olympic Games: A Critical Approach* (Bingley: Emerald Publishing, 2020), 111.
5 Andy Ross, "Adam Peaty to FINA: 'I Don't Care, Ban Me If You've Got To,' In Support of International Swim League." *Swimming World Magazine*, December 20, 2018, https://www.swimmingworldmagazine.com/news/adam-peaty-to-fina-i-dont-care-ban-me-if-youve-got-to-in-support-of-international-swim-league/.
6 "Shields v. Fed'n Internationale de Natation." Case No. 18-cv-07393-JSC, accessed at *Casetext*, https://casetext.com/case/shields-v-fedn-internationale-de-natation
7 John Gleaves and Matthew Llewellyn, "Ethics, Nationalism, and the Imagined Community: The Case Against Inter-National Sport," *Journal of the Philosophy of Sport* 41, no. 1 (2013): 1–19.
8 Ian Payten and Tom Decent, "Why Aussie Olympians aren't on board for Paris' floating opening ceremony," *The Sydney Morning Herald*, March 7, 2024, https://www.smh.com.au/sport/why-aussie-olympians-aren-t-on-board-for-paris-floating-opening-ceremony-20240307-p5falg.html.
9 Birgit Schönau, "Einer von ihnen," Süddeutsche Zeitung, May 10, 2010, https://www.sueddeutsche.de/sport/michael-schumacher-und-die-italiener-einer-von-ihnen-1.309017.
10 Philip Barker, "The Hidden Legacies of Moscow '80: Changes in Ceremonial and Attitudes," *Journal of Olympic History* 18, no. 2 (2010): 32–37.
11 "James Gilkes: A lost opportunity," *Sarbroek News*, August 15, 2018, https://www.stabroeknews.com/2008/08/15/opinion/editorial/james-gilkes-a-lost-opportunity/.
12 Samuel P. Huntington, *The Clash of Civilizations and the Remaking of World Order* (New York: Simon & Schuster, 1996).
13 "UN body questions French move to bar its athletes from wearing hijab at Paris 2024," *Reuters*, September 27, 2023, https://www.reuters.com/sports/un-body-questions-french-move-bar-its-athletes-wearing-hijab-paris-2024-2023-09-27/.
14 Bruce Kidd, "Psychological Aspects of the Experiences of Athletes in the Olympic Villages: Issues and Challenges," *Sport in Society* 16, no. 4 (2013): 482–90.
15 Jörg Krieger, "Fastest, highest, youngest? Analysing the athlete's experience of the Singapore Youth Olympic Games," *International Review for the Sociology of Sport* 48, no. 6 (2012): 706–719.

16 "Paris caters for Olympic romance by distributing 220,000 free condoms to athletes," *France 24*, March 20, 2023, https://www.france24.com/en/live-news/20240320-paris-caters-for-olympic-romance-with-220-000-free-condoms.
17 Hans Westerbeek and Rochelle Eime, "The Physical Activity and Sport Participation Framework – A Policy Model Toward Being Physically Active Across the Lifespan," *Frontiers in Sports and Active Living* 3, article np. 608593 (2021): 1–11.
18 "2020 Survey Results: Athletes rights, Athlete welfare, Athlete representation," *Global Athlete*, October 8, 2020, https://static1.squarespace.com/static/5c8a203ac46f6d6629eac1f4/t/5e4fecb29963cc36ec44b04f/1582296243015/Global+Athlete+Survey+Results+Rights+Welfare+Compensation.pdf.
19 Pierre de Coubertin, "The Philosophic Foundation of Modern Olympism", in *Olympism. Selected Writings*, ed. Norbert Müller (Lausanne: International Olympic Committee, 2000), 580–583.
20 Nicole Selmer and Almut Sülzle, "(En-)gendering the European football family: the changing discourse on women and gender at EURO 2008," in *Governance, Citizenship and the New European Football Championships*, eds. Wolfram Manzenreiter and Georg Spitaler (London: Routledge, 2012), 124–139.
21 Neil Ewen, "Team GB, or No Team GB, That Is The Question: Olympic Football and the Post-War Crisis of Britishness," *Sport in History* 32, no. 2 (2012): 302–324.
22 "INFINITY LEAGUE von DAZN: The New Way of Football," *DAZN*, May 26, 2024,
23 "Skill Challenge," *International Ice Hockey Federation*, n.d., https://webarchive.iihf.com/channels1415/hdc/skills-chall/index.html.

Index

For Product Safety Concerns and Information please contact our EU representative GPSR@taylorandfrancis.com
Taylor & Francis Verlag GmbH, Kaufingerstraße 24, 80331 München, Germany

www.ingramcontent.com/pod-product-compliance
Lightning Source LLC
LaVergne TN
LVHW010839120826
845149LV00017B/3308